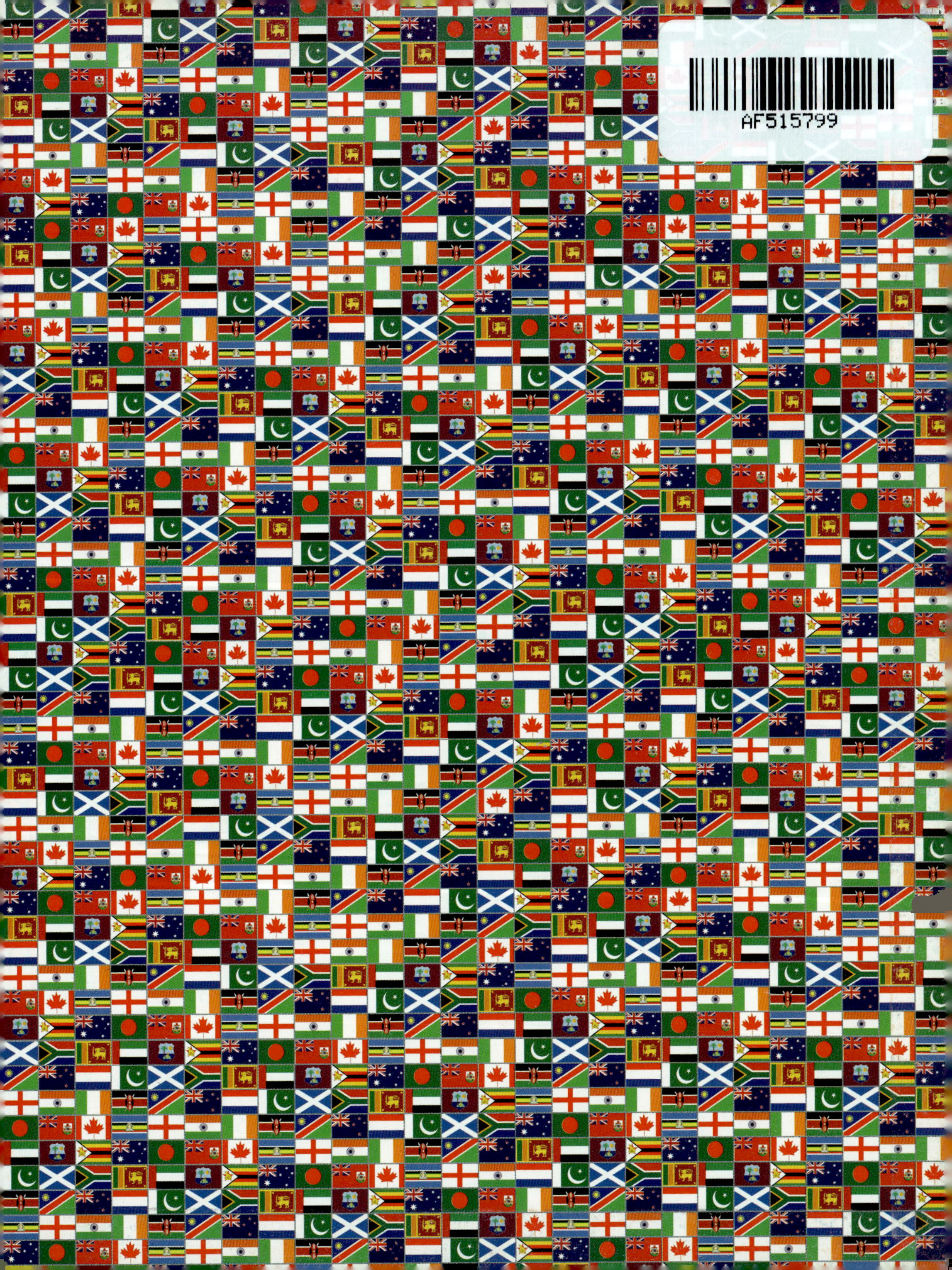

THE HISTORY OF WORLD CUP CRICKET
1975–2011

Sachin Tendulkar's bat

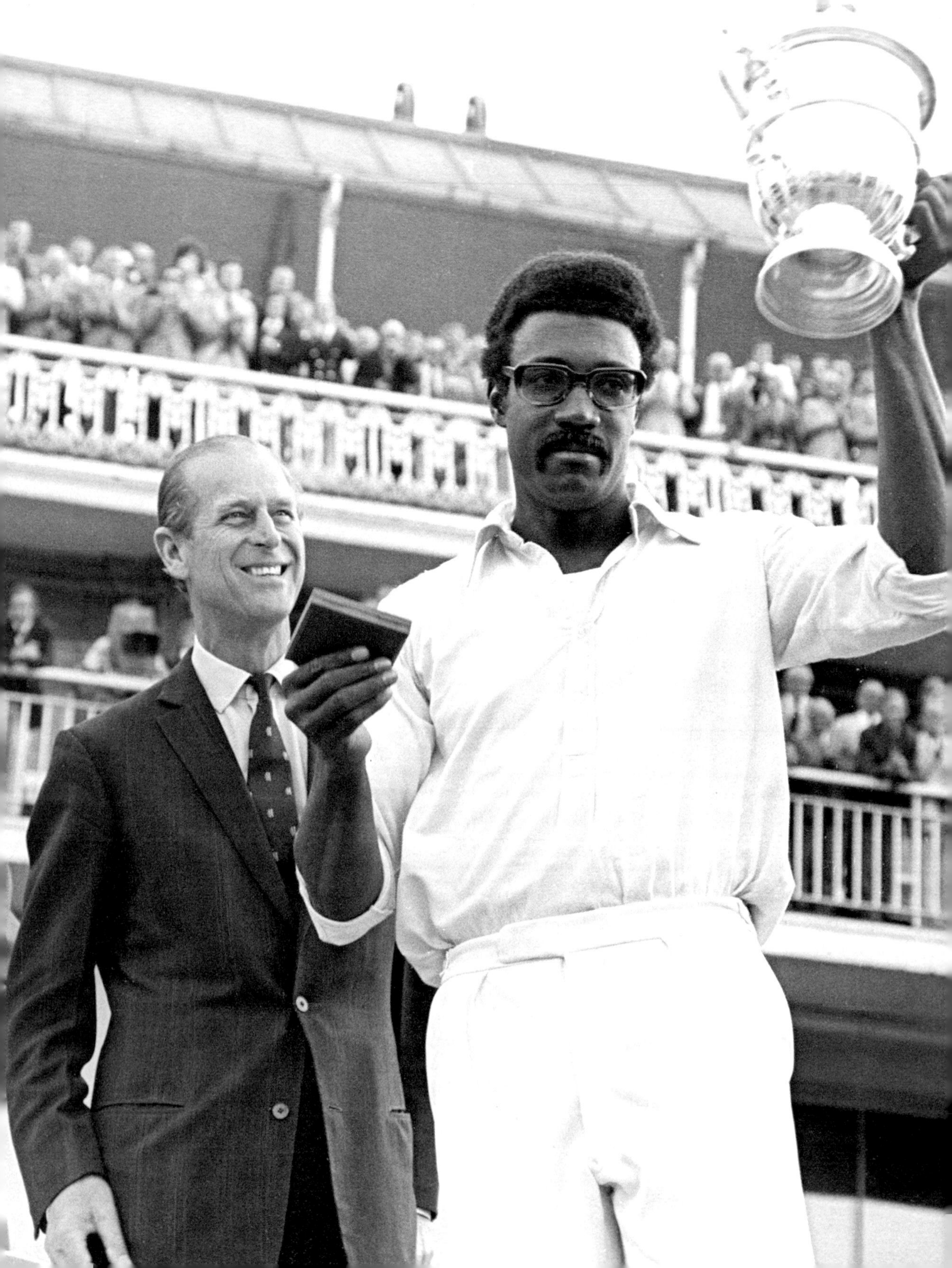

THE HISTORY OF WORLD CUP CRICKET

1975–2011

James Alter

1975 World Cup Final: Prince Philip with Clive Lloyd, captain of the winning West Indies team

Lustre Press
Roli Books

ISBN: 978-81-7436-841-6

First published in India in 2011.

Roli Books Pvt Ltd
M-75, Greater Kailash II Market
New Delhi 110 048
Phone: ++91 (011) 4068 2000
Fax: ++91 (011) 2921 7185

E-mail: info@rolibooks.com
Website: www.rolibooks.com

Also at
Bangalore, Chennai, Jaipur,
Varanasi & Mumbai

Editor: Priyanka Nath
Design: Bonita Vaz-Shimray
Layout: Sanjeev Mathpal
Production: Shaji Sahadevan, Jyoti Dey

Printed in India.

Front cover: Sachin Tendulkar hits a boundary during the 2003 World Cup (Getty Images)

Foreword

WOW, cricket is growing up. It seems only recently that Clive Lloyd was playing a landmark innings at Lord's, and already the tenth edition is upon us. And yet, it has travelled much in the human landscape. In 1975, indeed even in 1979, it was like a long tea party. It got over in two weeks, just as people had begun to warm up towards the idea of its arrival, and there were four matches every playing day. One-day cricket had few supporters; certainly, no one dreamt that it would be a messiah, that it would one day become the financial giant that would prop test cricket up.

It was appropriate that the first World Cup was played in what was then believed to be the home of cricket. It is just as appropriate that, at another crucial hour in its history, the one-day World Cup returns to a land that is very different to its original abode, but home nonetheless. But today, as in 1975, one-day cricket faces an uncertain future.

There is much riding on World Cup 2011. T20 cricket has done to 50-overs cricket what the one-day international had done to the existing form years ago. The ODI is no longer the revolutionary, but the establishment seeking to protect its turf from a new invader. The world is unrecognizable from the time the ODI announced itself; newer generations are snappier, more demanding, less respectful. Fifty-over cricket cannot use its legacy, however bright, to demand attention for itself. It must prove itself.

That is why for the one-day international to survive, or at any rate to remain strong, it is imperative that this World Cup be a roaring success; not financially, but in terms of the quality of the cricket played and the number of people who watch it. The last edition in the West Indies was buffeted by harsh winds and was largely forgettable.

Interestingly, unlike most recent World Cups, World Cup 2011 is wide open for takers. Australia have owned it since 1999, but can no longer claim permanent tenancy rights. They have slipped alarmingly in the last twelve months and, while they still have the people to win it, they will surprise many if they do. Undoubtedly, South Africa must believe that their time has arrived that they have acknowledged the existence of spinners and have a side that is truly balanced in all conditions. Pakistan have much to prove and they remain unpredictable as ever; indeed the smaller the game, the more likely they are to win it.

India will believe this is their best chance for a long time. They have the batting; the bowlers suitable for these conditions; a captain who is widely respected; and a legend who is hungry, never having tasted success. They must be in a short list of three or four teams to win the Cup.

Irrespective of what happens, this World Cup will add to the legend of the event. There have been many great moments and they are well captured in this book. Indeed, it was at one such unforgettable moment that I first met the author of this book. Australia had just beaten South Africa and progressed to the final via a tied result at Birmingham in a wonderful cricket match, the crowd had gathered around the pavilion, when, from my in-vision position, I spotted a man I have greatly admired over the years, the actor Tom Alter. There is sport on every square millimetre of Tom's body, and on this day, he introduced me to a bright, excited young man. 'This is my son,' he said, and today, it is that son, James Alter, who brings this book to you.

Harsha Bhogle
Mumbai
January 2011

Preface

EACH of us has our own memories of every World Cup; the men and moments that defined a particular tournament, as well as the time each of us were at in our lives. For me, personally, the 1996 World Cup will forever be associated with an awakening to cricket, both emotionally and physically, as I returned to boarding school for high school. A little over three years later, the 1999 World Cup rolled around all too soon as I prepared to graduate high school and step out of my comfort zone. The year 2003 saw me studying in the US, trying to juggle studies with arranging for a cable dish to watch the World Cup; and in 2007, I was a professional journalist getting paid to watch the World Cup and write match reports and ball-by-ball commentary on the Internet. Each tournament brought happiness as well as sadness, and there were countless innings, catches and moments that created an unforgettable mosaic.

Roli Books' A History of the Cricket World Cup is an attempt at reproducing the memories of the nine previous World Cups, through text and photographs, and compiles a companion for fans of the great game of cricket.

Reproduced accurately in the following pages are brief scorecards of each World Cup match played from 1975 to 2007, as well as brief summaries of each semi-final and final, and highlights of memorable matches and moments during each of the nine tournaments held so far. There is a vast and impressive array of photographs to both supplement those moments and relive the memories.

A highlight of the book is the special World Cup walkthrough section at the end of certain chapters. Featured here are the memories of legends including Dickie Bird, the legendary umpire who officiated in three World Cup finals, starting from the inaugural edition; Roger Binny, the highest wicket-taker of the 1983 World Cup; Geoff Marsh, whose batting and starts with David Boon played a big role in Australia's maiden World Cup win in 1987; Geoff Allott, whose 20 wickets in 1999 broke the tournament record and helped a spirited New Zealand side reach the semi-finals; Andy Bichel, whose role in Australia's 2003 triumph – spectacularly against England and New Zealand – was so crucial; and Matthew Hayden, who broke the Cup record for most runs in a tournament in 2007.

Also included is the complete World Cup 2011 schedule, which you can pull out and keep as your ready reference before and through World Cup 2011. All information contained in this book is correct to the best of my knowledge and updated at the time of going to press. Any errors or omissions are purely inadvertent.

I sincerely hope that fans of this exhilarating game, especially in times when the fifty-over game has come under much criticism, find this book a handy companion and an enjoyable read as they roll back the years in the build-up to the 2011 World Cup.

Yours in sport,

James Alter
Mumbai
January 2011

Opposite page: Mike Gatting reverse-sweeps during the 1987 final at Eden Gardens

To the cricket teams of
Woodstock School
1998-99 and
the College of Wooster
2002-03

Acknowledgment

I wish to first thank Roli Books for their interest in the book and their editorial comments. Hopefully my work justified their interest and efforts. Their team worked to a tight deadline to bring out a book that shows no sign of having been produced so quickly.

Needless to say, the cooperation of all those players and officials connected to the various World Cup tournaments down the years is greatly appreciated. I benefitted much from the cooperation and comments of these individuals during research for this book. Speaking to them was an invaluable first-hand experience.

Nagraj Gollapudi, Sidharth Monga, Sriram Veera and Brydon Coverdale need to be thanked for accommodating many of my last minute unreasonable demands. Finally, thanks to my mother for allowing me the space to work, my father for his advice and Meha for helping keep me on course throughout this project.

1992 World Cup: England v South Africa, Melbourne. View of the Melbourne Cricket Ground

Contents

1975 | **England** | Lloyd of London 13

1979 | **England** | King Richards' Rule 23

1983 | **England** | No Lording It over India 35

1987 | **India & Pakistan** | Border's Skirmish 47

1992 | **Australia & New Zealand** | A Khan Job 59

1996 | **India, Pakistan & Sri Lanka** | Sheer Lanka 71

1999 | **England, Scotland, Ireland & Netherlands** | We Warned You 87

2003 | **South Africa, Zimbabwe & Kenya** | Aus-some 103

2007 | **West Indies** | Blizzard of Oz 121

Records and Statistics 136

1975 England

The crowd at the end of the final between Australia and West Indies at Lord's

Lloyd of London

JUST four years from the time the first limited-overs international was held at the hallowed Melbourne Cricket Ground, the inaugural World Cup, known as the Prudential Cup, marked the debut of the premier one-day international (ODI) tournament. It was held in England between 7 June and 21 June 1975; contested between eight teams; and won by West Indies, the most outstanding performers of the tournament.

The Prudential World Cup had matches consisting 60 overs per side. The preliminary matches were played in two groups of four teams and, initially, league matches were played within individual groups. The top two teams from each group played the semi-finals, and the winners of these were pitted against each other for the final. In all, 15 matches were played. Unlike today, players wore a traditional white uniform and red balls were used. There were no night games as well.

Eight countries participated in the event: Australia, England, India, New Zealand, West Indies, Sri Lanka, Pakistan, and East Africa (comprising players from Kenya, Tanzania, Uganda and Zambia). A notable omission from the tournament was the South African cricket team, which was not competing due to the international sports boycott.

The first World Cup began with England batting first and posting a record 334 for 4, then the highest score for a 60-over game in the country. The first World Cup delivery was bowled by India's Madan Lal to England's opener John Jameson, who happened to have been born in Bombay. Dennis Amiss scored England's first century, and in reply to a mammoth total, India pottered around – literally, with Sunil Gavaskar batting 60 overs for 36 – and finished on 132 for 3. Teams remained unsure of how to approach batting in the 60-over format and on such a grand stage, but thankfully the remaining league matches weren't as mind-numbing as the tournament opener.

The semi-finals were played between England and Australia and New Zealand and West Indies. In the final played at Lord's, West Indies beat Australia by 17 runs in a great match. Clive Lloyd, the West Indies captain, was declared the Man of the Final for an outstanding 85-ball 102.

The tournament was a success both on and off the field. Thousands of spectators thronged the eight venues in fine weather to help the organizers collect £188, 598 from gate money. Prudent Insurance Company, the tournament sponsor, had pumped in £100,000, including £9,000 in prize money.

Opposite page: Clive Lloyd's century in the 1975 final was one for the ages

GROUP A: ENGLAND, INDIA, NEW ZEALAND AND EAST AFRICA

GROUP B: WEST INDIES, AUSTRALIA, PAKISTAN AND SRI LANKA

1975 Prudential World Cup statistics

Formats Round robin and Knockout
Host England
Champions West Indies (first title)
Participants 8
Matches played 15
Attendance 158,000 (10,533 per match)
Most runs Glenn Turner (333)
Most wickets Gary Gilmour (11)

Rodney Marsh was adjudged the best wicketkeeper for nine catches and a stumping.

Imran Khan took time off from captaining Oxford to play in the first of his five World Cups.

Alvin Kallicharran hooks during his devastating innings against Australia

Pakistan v West Indies

11 June

Eighth match, Birmingham

WEST INDIES were facing defeat on 203 for 9, chasing Pakistan's formidable 266 for 7 off 60 overs. Deryck Murray was joined by Andy Roberts and the pair began their Houdini Act. Murray held up one end resolutely, while pinching singles; and Roberts chanced his arm with some proficient hitting. With two balls to go, Roberts turned a Wasim Raja delivery for the winning run and a West Indian stampede followed. Tears of joy flowed unabated and that magical moment proved to be the catalyst for West Indies' eventual success in the tournament.

India v New Zealand

14 June

Tenth match, Manchester

GLENN TURNER was in supreme form during the Prudential Cup. In all, he scored two hundreds in the four games New Zealand featured in during the tournament, en route to 333 runs at an outstanding average of 166.50, with a strike rate of 68.51. A week after he carried his bat for an unbeaten 171 against East Africa, Turner changed gear to nurse New Zealand through a tense chase for 231 against India. His unbeaten 114 off 177 balls with 13 boundaries helped New Zealand win in the 59th over.

Australia v West Indies

14 June

Eleventh match, The Oval, London

HAVING narrowly escaped defeat against Pakistan, West Indies got their mojo together against Australia at The Oval, where Alvin Kallicharran's 78 included a savage attack on Dennis Lillee. A marquee event saw Australia recover from 61 for 5 on an overcast morning to 192, which a rampant West Indies chased down with seven wickets and 14 overs remaining. Roy Fredericks began like a loose train, clobbering Dennis Lillee and Jeff Thomson in an innings in which his cutting and hooking was awesome. With Kallicharran, Fredericks put on 124; Kallicharran was in sublime form, hitting a six and thirteen fours in his innings. Most memorable was his assault on Lillee, off whom he scored 35 off his last ten balls faced. Needless to say, Australia were hammered.

Dennis Amiss scored ODI cricket's first century in the first World Cup match.

England v Australia

18 June, First semi-final, Leeds

AUSTRALIA'S Gary Gilmour burst onto the scene at Headingley in June 1975 when, in ideal conditions, he destroyed England in a display rated by *Wisden* as the greatest one-day bowling performance ever. Gilmour had previously been Australia's 12th man throughout the preliminary matches, but was suddenly asked, ahead of Jeff Thomson, to share the new ball with Dennis Lillee. 'I only found out as we were going out on the field,' he once said. 'You never knew with Ian Chappell what was going to happen until it happened.' On the field, Gilmour produced a classic left arm seamer's spell to reduce England to 52 for 8. Three of his victims were caught behind, two went LWB and one, the captain Mike Denness, was bowled through the gate by a gem that nipped back in. In all, Gilmour had extraordinary figures of 12-6-14-6. Later, chasing just 94, Australia were staring down the barrel at 38 for 6, but Gilmour's run-a-ball 28 brought them home in a fantastic all-round performance.

New Zealand v West Indies

18 June, Second semi-final, The Oval, London

ANOTHER Man-of-the-Match award for Alvin Kallicharran, whose 72 from 92 balls sealed a five-wicket win for West Indies. New Zealand had struggled from the time Clive Lloyd inserted them as West Indies' pace attack hustled and bounced them into submission and a total of 158 in 52.2 overs. Glenn Turner was forced to battle for a dogged 36, but with nobody apart from him and Geoff Howarth putting up much of a fight, New Zealand lost nine wickets for 64 runs after lunch. Kallicharran and Gordon Greenidge smashed a 125-run stand for the second wicket, with the diminutive Kallicharran savaging Dayle Hadlee's short-ball tactics.

THE FINALS Australia v West Indies

21 June, Lord's, London

CLIVE LLOYD played one of the greatest innings in the history of one-day cricket at the first World Cup final. Put in to bat, West Indies were reeling at 50 for 3 when the skipper joined Rohan Kanhai. In an awesome display of power hitting, Lloyd raced to his 100 of 82 balls, blasting twelve fours and two sixes as West Indies amassed a winning total of 291 for 9 off 60 overs. For a hundred and eight unforgettable batting minutes, Lloyd was the King of Lord's on that long summer day.

There was much action during the second innings. Viv Richards' had failed with the bat, but made a stunning impact with his fielding, running out three huge wickets. First to go was the opener Alan Turner for 40; then a direct hit nailed Greg Chappell; and when Ian Chappell was found short by a beautiful pick-up and flick, Australia were wobbling.

Later, as Australia's last-wicket pair attempted a memorable heist, Dennis Lillee slapped a no-ball from Vanburn Holder straight to Roy Fredericks at extra cover. The crowd missed the call and rushed on, thinking that West Indies had won. Fredericks tried another run-out, only to see the ball vanish into the throng. 'Keep running,' shouted Lillee to Jeff Thompson. When order was restored, umpires Dickie Bird and Tom Spencer declared they could have two runs. 'Pig's arse,' cried Thompson. 'We've been running up and down here all afternoon!' So the pair was granted three.

Ultimately, West Indies went on to win the match by 17 runs amidst the uninhibited joy of Caribbean supporters.

Sunil Gavaskar's 36 against England at Lord's is the slowest innings in any World Cup.

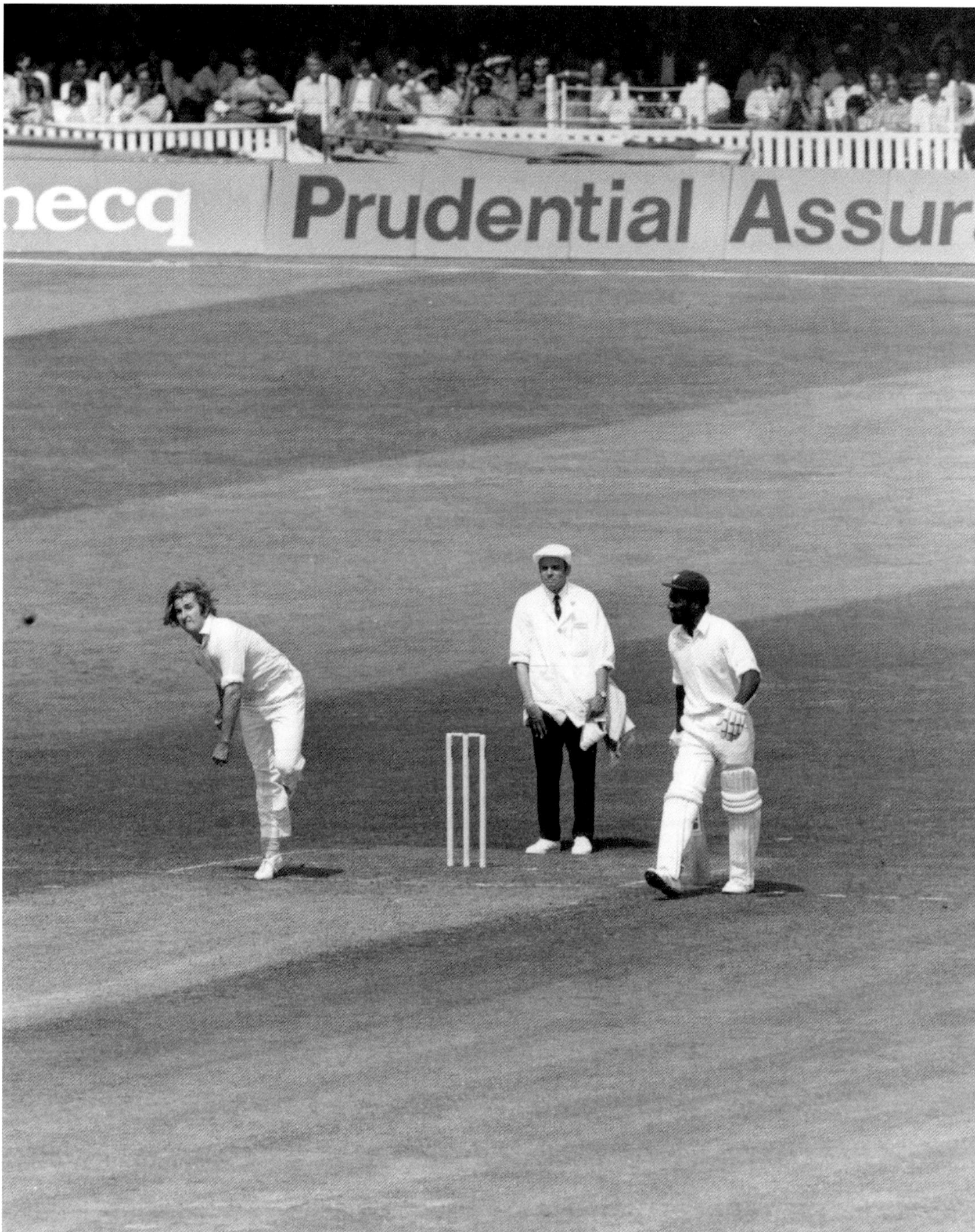

Bishan Singh Bedi returned the most economical spell in a World Cup match – 12-8-6-1.

'Somebody nicked my hat!'

Dickie Bird

Officiated in three World Cup finals, beginning in 1975

THE 1975 Prudential World Cup was a spectacle, because a tournament like this hadn't been attempted before. One-day cricket, or 60-over cricket as it was back then, had been in existence for four years, but not all of the teams were equipped to succeed in the format. There was that match between England and India, the first game of the tournament, where in the second innings, India crawled their way to less than half of the target. Wasn't the best match to showcase the event, but India got better and the matches were also markedly better as the tournament progressed.

The fans took to the matches in a good way. Most grounds got good crowds and whenever England or West Indies played, it was a full house. I stood in four matches during the World Cup and they were all good matches. I remember officiating during Glenn Turner's 171 not out, India's victory over East Africa, and a good match between West Indies and Australia. Lovely batting from Alvin Kallicharran in that match; proper batsman he was, really good to watch.

The 1975 World Cup final was the best one-day game I ever stood in. Two champion sides, with some great players, in a great match at Lord's. And it was a lovely day as well. I arrived at the ground at 7:30 in the morning and left at 10:00 at night. Play began at 11:00, and it wasn't till around 09:00 that the Duke of Edinburgh presented Clive Lloyd the Prudential World Cup trophy. It was a proper English midsummer's day, with bursts of sunshine followed by twilight, and to drive out of Lord's after an unforgettable day's cricket was a special feeling and one I won't forget.

On the field, we were treated to a fabulous century from Lloyd – what a player! – and some brilliant fielding from both sides. The Australians had fielded really well all tournament – I recall Ian Chappell taking some sharp catches and doing well in the field also – but on this day at Lord's, it was Viv Richard who stole the show. He hadn't done too much in England but on this day he was electric. He ran out three batsmen, including Chappell, and that's where the final was won. Unforgettable pick-ups and throws, just smack on the mark. Chappell's run-out was the one that turned it West Indies's way; Chappell poked the ball towards midwicket and set off, but then stopped momentarily as he saw Richards run in. Then Richards fumbled and Chappell set off again, running like a rocket to the other end, but Richards' throw was dead straight to Lloyd, who did the rest. Absolutely cracking fielding from Richards that day.

There was some confusion at the end of the match, which was also unforgettable. The Australian last pair of Jeff Thomson and Dennis Lillee was batting, and at one stage, the ball was played down to fine leg. The throw came in to Deryck Murray who broke the stumps and the fans thought the match was over, so they spilled onto the field. I'm talking about thousands of fans, cheering and yelling, running towards us. I was scared! But I hadn't ruled it out, and when they realized, it took a while to file them off the ground. We kept shooing them away but there were thousands.

There was more chaos. Thomson popped a catch to a fielder on the off side and the fans didn't hear the call for no-ball. Again they poured onto the field like a mad mob and we all had to find cover. I was swatting people away and somebody even nicked my hat! Utter chaos, but somehow we all managed to clear the fans off the field – literally, because they stood virtually on the boundary ropes – and the match was over soon after. What a day!

Opposite page: Dickie Bird officiates during the World Cup final at Lord's

Gary Gilmour was the bowler of the tournament, taking 11 wickets in two appearances.

SUMMARY OF RESULTS

GROUP STAGE

Group A: East Africa v New Zealand at Birmingham – 7 June New Zealand won by 181 runs. New Zealand 309-5 (60 ov); East Africa 128-8 (60 ov)	Group A: East Africa v India at Leeds – 11 June India won by 10 wickets. East Africa 120 (55.3 ov); India 123-0 (29.5 ov)	Group A: England v East Africa at Birmingham – 14 June England won by 196 runs. England 290-5 (60 ov); East Africa 94 (52.3 ov)
Group A: England v India at Lord's – 7 June England won by 202 runs. England 334-4 (60 ov); India 132-3 (60 ov)	Group A: England v New Zealand at Nottingham – 11 June England won by 80 runs. England 266-6 (60 ov); New Zealand 186 (60 ov)	Group A: India v New Zealand at Manchester – 14 June New Zealand won by 4 wickets. India 230 (60 ov); New Zealand 233-6 (58.5 ov)
Group B: Australia v Pakistan at Leeds – 7 June Australia won by 73 runs. Australia 278-7 (60 ov); Pakistan 205 (53 ov)	Group B: Australia v Sri Lanka at The Oval – 11 June Australia won by 52 runs. Australia 328-5 (60 ov); Sri Lanka 276-4 (60 ov)	Group B: Australia v West Indies at The Oval – 14 June West Indies won by 7 wickets. Australia 192 (53.4 ov); West Indies 195-3 (46 ov)
Group B: Sri Lanka v West Indies at Manchester – 7 June West Indies won by 9 wickets. Sri Lanka 86 (37.2 ov); West Indies 87-1 (20.4 ov)	Group B: Pakistan v West Indies at Birmingham – 11 June West Indies won by 1 wicket. Pakistan 266-7 (60 ov); West Indies 267-9 (59.4 ov)	Group B: Pakistan v Sri Lanka at Nottingham – 14 June Pakistan won by 192 runs. Pakistan 330-6 (60 ov); Sri Lanka 138 (50.1 ov)

The combined teams assemble behind the pavilion at Lord's

SUMMARY OF RESULTS

GROUP A					
TEAM	POINTS	PLAYED	WON	LOSS	RUN RATE
England	12	3	3	0	4.94
New Zealand	8	3	2	1	4.07
India	4	3	1	2	3.24
East Africa	0	3	0	3	1.90

GROUP B					
TEAM	POINTS	PLAYED	WON	LOSS	RUN RATE
West Indies	12	3	3	0	4.35
Australia	8	3	2	1	4.43
Pakistan	–	3	1	2	4.45
Sri Lanka	0	3	0	3	2.78

Umpire Bill Alley looks on as New Zealand's Hedley Howarth bowls

1ST SEMI-FINAL

England v Australia at Leeds – 18 June
Australia won by 4 wickets.
England 93 (36.2 ov);
Australia 94-6 (28.4 ov)

2ND SEMI-FINAL

New Zealand v West Indies at The Oval – 18 June
West Indies won by 5 wickets.
New Zealand 158 (52.2 ov);
West Indies 159-5 (40.1 ov)

FINAL

Australia v West Indies at Lord's – 21 June
West Indies won by 17 runs.
West Indies 291-8 (60 ov);
Australia 274 (58.4 ov)

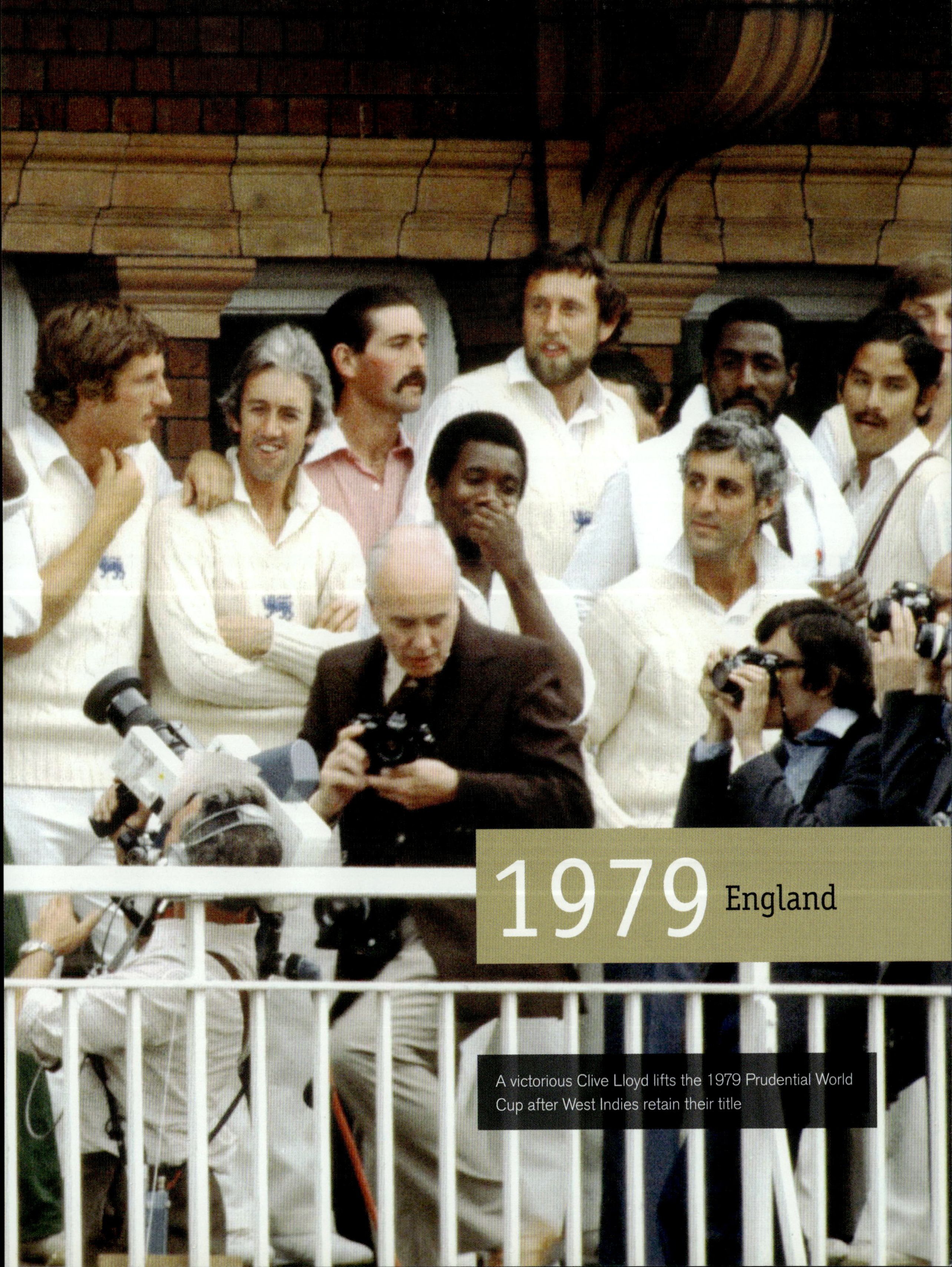

1979 England

A victorious Clive Lloyd lifts the 1979 Prudential World Cup after West Indies retain their title

King Richards' Rule

THE weather wasn't as shiny as it had been four years ago – Sri Lanka was washed out at The Oval before even a ball could be bowled; and England v Canada played out across two days at Old Trafford – but the Prudential Cup was a success from 9 June to 23 June.

West Indies arrived in England as favourites to retain their title, which they duly did, having included all those contracted to Kerry Packer's World Series Cricket. Pakistan opted to do the same, but Australia didn't, and included a series of virtually unknown players, for which they paid the price. West Indies were ahead from the start. South Africa were yet again ignored for the showpiece event, owing to apartheid. And so to make up the numbers, a separate tournament called the ICC Trophy was held, and from it emerged two minor teams: Sri Lanka and Canada.

India floundered for the second World Cup running, while New Zealand's band of bits-and-pieces players carried them into the semi-finals. England won all their league matches, including a low-scorer at Headingley, while Pakistan also qualified. Half-centuries to Mike Brearley and Graham Gooch outdid New Zealand at Old Trafford, though just by nine runs, while at The Oval, West Indies overcame a bout of jitters, thanks to some canny bowling from Viv Richards, to enter their second final.

West Indies defeated hosts England by 92 runs in the final at Lord's on June 23. While Clive Lloyd had smashed the title-winning century four years ago at the same venue, it was Viv Richards who emulated his captain in 1979, smashing eleven boundaries and three sixes on his way to an unbeaten 138 off 157 balls. Starring alongside Richards was Collis King, who slammed 86 from 66 balls. Chasing a mammoth 287, England's openers Brearley and Geoffrey Boycott used up more than half their overs in compiling a 129-run stand, and left too much for the rest of the batting line-up. Joel Garner was at his menacing best, mixing vicious yorkers with short stuff, and collected 5 for 36 as England slid from 183 for 2 to 194 all out.

For their success, West Indies received the Prudential Cup and £10,000; England, runners-up, £4,000. Richards pocketed the Man-of-the-Match award and £300. Prize money amounted to £25,900. As in 1975, the Prudential Assurance Company put in the money, except this time, two and a half times as much. Gate receipts came to £359,700, almost double the £188,000 for the inaugural competition and the surplus of £350,000 was shared between the full and associate members of the International Cricket Conference.

Opposite page: England had no answer to Viv Richards during the 1979 final at Lord's

GROUP A: ENGLAND, PAKISTAN, AUSTRALIA AND CANADA

GROUP B: WEST INDIES, INDIA, NEW ZEALAND AND SRI LANKA

1979 Prudential World Cup statistics

Formats Round robin and Knockout

Host England

Champions West Indies (second title)

Participants 8

Matches played 15

Attendance 132,000 (8,800 per match)

Most runs Gordon Greenidge (253)

Most wickets Mike Hendrick (10)

In 1979, only two centuries were scored, marking this as the lowest scoring World Cup.

Viv Richards is the only person to have played World Cup football and World Cup cricket.

HIGHLIGHTS

England v Australia

9 June

Third match, Lord's, London

A full house of 25,000 witnessed the home side beat their old rivals with ease. Australia began watchfully after being asked to bat on a gloomy morning, reaching 56 in 21 overs before Bob Willis snapped the obdurate stand in his second spell. From here, the Australians found the going tough against a tidy pace attack, and it was the surprise introduction of Geoffrey Boycott and his gentle medium-pace that really turned the tables. Andrew Hilditch dragged the ball onto his stumps and Kim Hughes flicked to midwicket, setting in motion a collapse that included four run-outs. England had a few tense moments in a chase of 161, especially when two wickets fell for five runs, but Graham Gooch and Mike Brearley's 108-run stand eased nerves and set up a comfortable win.

Pakistan's Majid Khan clips to leg during the semi-finals
Opposite page: Collis King drives Graham Gooch during his onslaught at Lord's

India v Sri Lanka

16-18 June

Ninth match, Manchester

MAKING their debut at the World Cup, minnows Sri Lanka started with a memorable win over India at Old Trafford. It was the only win by an associate member of the ICC in the competition, and was richly deserved. That it came without the Sri Lankan captain Anura Tenekoon, who damaged a hamstring the previous day during training, was all the more commendable. Starring with the bat were Sunil Wettimuny, Roy Dias and Duleep Mendis (who hit an unbeaten 64 from 57 balls), as Sri Lanka made 238 for 5. After an obligatory rest day, India fell apart from a strong start against a gutsy spin attack. Mendis was named Man of the Match.

England v Pakistan

11 June

Twelfth match, Leeds

A closely-fought encounter went England's way, thanks largely to Mike Hendricks and an exciting spell of 4 for 3 in eight balls. Asif Iqbal put England in and they were quickly 2 for 4; Geoffrey Boycott did what he knew best, batting 85 minutes for a crucial partnership with Graham Gooch. Then Majid Khan's offbreaks snared three wickets, and England slumped to 118 for 8. The two Bobs, Taylor and Willis, combined to forge what would be a match-winning stand of 43 and got the total to 165 for 9. Pakistan began cautiously, but Hendricks' crafty cutters pulled them back from 27 for 0 to 34 for 6. Asif and Wasim Raja fought valiantly for nearly two hours until Bob Willis returned to the captain, and Mike Brearley again turned to Boycott. With his cap turned backwards, Boycott grabbed 2 for 14 at the death, when he lured Sikander Bakht into a brainless swipe while Imran Khan was winning the game at the other end. This convinced England to go with four main bowlers for the rest of their matches.

England's win over Canada with 277 balls in hand is the sixth-largest victory margin.

The 129-run partnership of Mike Brearley and Geoff Boycott was the highest WC opening stand.

THE SEMI-FINALS

England v New Zealand

20 June, First semi-final, Manchester

THE first semi-final was a great game played out in front of a capacity of 22,000 at Old Trafford, with England beating New Zealand by nine runs. In a game that ebbed and flowed marvellously, New Zealand's spirited attack began well, but was put to task by Mike Brearley and Graham Gooch up the order, with Ian Botham, and Derek Randall later contributing important cameos to get the total to 221. New Zealand replied with a 47-run stand between John Wright and Bruce Edgar in 16 overs. As wickets fell around him, Wright (69 from 137) did a similar job as Gooch had before he was run out. Despite the presence of so many all-rounders, New Zealand fell nine runs short.

Pakistan v West Indies

22 June, Second semi-final, The Oval, London

BATHED in sunshine, a crowd of 20,000 witnessed red-hot West Indies brush aside Pakistan. Asif Iqbal's decision to field came a cropper as the West Indies openers put on 132, with Sarfraz Nawaz having an off day; in all, he bled 71 from his quota. Asif claimed four wickets, including the top order, upon whose efforts West Indies had thrived. A total of 293 for 6 would prove too much for Pakistan, who despite a marvellous partnership of 166 in 36 overs between the effervescent pair of Majid Khan and Zaheer Abbas lost their middle order to Viv Richards' gentle offerings after the pair had been removed by Colin Croft. 'I was wrong to put West Indies in to bat in on an excellent batting track,' felt Asif years later. 'That decision probably cost us a spot in the final.'

Opposite page: England captain Mike Brearley during England's cautious reply in the final

THE FINALS England v West Indies

23 June, Lord's, London

BATTING first, West Indies were reeling at 99 for 4, when Collis King joined Viv Richards, the pre-eminent batsman of his time. As he reached the middle, Richards offered him some advice with lunch soon to be taken. 'Hey man, take it easy ... we have plenty of time.' King, however, wasn't thinking along those lines. 'Smokey,' he replied, 'I ain't gonna let Geoffrey [Boycott] get this man. In the league there would be no mercy, so why should this be any different?' In the next 21 overs, some ferocious hitting from King and Richards silenced the home support and turned Lord's into a Caribbean carnival. King smacked 86 off 67 balls, with ten fours and two sixes, and Richards stroked an excellent 138, as West Indies amassed 286 for 9 in 60 overs. The pair had added 139 in 77 minutes of carnage. The last over of the innings was bowled by Mike Hendrick, whose 11 previous overs had cost 36. Richards was on strike and on 124, and after six deliveries, he had moved to 138, having swung the final delivery over square leg for six.

Then it was over to Joel Garner, who annihilated England for 194 after a dour opening partnership of 129 between Mike Brearley and Geoff Boycott. That alliance had eaten up too many overs and the asking rate was touching double digits. 'We were grateful to England for their tactics,' recalled Joel Garner years later, 'by the time they [the openers] were gone it would have taken a superhuman effort to retrieve situation.' This was humility at its best, because what Garner did next was pretty superhuman. Coming back into the attack in the forty-eighth over, with the late-afternoon gloom setting in, the 6'8" Garner pelted in and knocked the stuffing out of England with a series of crushing yorkers. Graham Gooch went first ball, David Gower three deliveries later, and in his following over, Garner cleaned up the tail. In 11 deliveries, he had seized 5 for 4, and England had lost their last eight wickets for 11 runs. 'Garner broke the back,' Clive Lloyd said. 'It was just wonderful.' Garner's figures were the best in a World Cup final.

In the 1979 World Cup final, five Englishmen were dismissed for a duck – a world record.

1979

‘I didn’t want to die there’

Sir Vivian Richards
1979 World Cup winner
(as told to CNN-IBN’s *Champions of the World*)

I have always prided myself on delivering when it matters, when the going gets tough. There are some of us who get weak when the occasion gets big. I always wanted to prove that I was not in that lane of also-rans. It was an opportunity and I was filled by enormous confidence. Was I nervous? Yeah, a little bit. Anyone who tells you that he is not even a little bit nervous before he approaches the crease is lying. A little nervousness helps you become a little more conscious about what needs to be achieved. It means your mind is on the prize and you know that this is what it’s all about.

I was confident that day at Lord’s. I’d played some of the preliminary matches and the confidence that I would have gained since 1975 made me even bigger and stronger. I really enjoyed the feeling of being in the final. It was a day of happiness for me. I wanted to go a step further. I felt that there was no use of being there and not knowing what that dance floor was all about. I wanted to test that dance floor if I was given an opportunity to do so. Everyone knows you need a little element of luck in order to achieve certain milestones in life and in cricket, and on that day, I just went in and tried to do what I knew best with the confidence I had. I didn’t want to die there. I wanted to make a statement that I could make some contribution with my bat to my team.

A lot of people have said and written that Collis King, with whom I forged that special partnership, had the audacity to upstage Viv Richards. I didn’t mind that at all. I was so happy that he came in and played the way he did. I was under enormous pressure after we lost early wickets. Gordon Greenidge and Desmond Haynes were back inside. Alvin Kallicharran and Clive Lloyd went back. I couldn’t afford to attack the bowling; I had to be careful and try to build partnerships.

Opposite page: Viv Richards’ excellent century in the final earned him the Man-of-the-Match award

If it wasn’t for Collis King, I wouldn’t have been able to play the way I did. I was thinking more conservatively than positively. But Collis entered and took the England bowling apart. I stayed at one end and thoroughly enjoyed his batting. I applauded every shot he played. That partnership set the tone for us to score 286.

I’m not quite sure about the so-called ‘strategy’ that people talk of during England’s slow reply to our total, when our captain supposedly dropped Geoffrey Boycott on purpose. I was bowling at the time, if I remember correctly, and Boycott used to say things like, ‘If you get my wicket, man, I will stop playing cricket’. That’s how he used to talk while batting. He would rub me about how poor my bowling was at the time. It was Clive Lloyd, who was fielding at midwicket, and Boycott chipped one and it was just about going over Clive’s head. Clive made an enormous leap, got his right hand on the ball, and just as he was about to fall, the ball fell into his lap and rolled out. I didn’t see the funny side of that!

Then it was all over to Joel Garner, whom I’d had the opportunity to play with at Somerset. I knew what he was capable of. I ended up getting the Man-of-the-Match award but there should have been another award, for Joel. That was a magnificent spell. Joel rode in and hit the stumps harder than anything I’d seen. It was such a magnificent feeling and I just felt that such a spell deserved much more than just a spell in a World Cup final. That spell never gave England a chance to come back in.

SUMMARY OF RESULTS

GROUP STAGE

Group B: India v West Indies
at Birmingham – 9 June
West Indies won by 9 wickets.
India 190 (53.1 ov);
West Indies 194-1 (51.3 ov)

Group B: West Indies v Sri Lanka
at The Oval – 13-15 June
Match abandoned without
a ball being bowled.

Group B: India v Sri Lanka
at Manchester – 16, 18 June
Sri Lanka won by 47 runs.
Sri Lanka 238-5 (60 ov);
India 191 (54.1 ov)

Group B: New Zealand v Sri Lanka
at Nottingham – 9 June
New Zealand won by 9 wickets.
Sri Lanka 189 (56.5 ov);
New Zealand 190-1 (47.4 ov)

Group B: India v New Zealand
at Leeds –13 June
New Zealand won by 8 wickets.
India 182 (55.5 ov);
New Zealand 183-2 (57 ov)

Group B: New Zealand v West Indies
at Nottingham – 16 June
West Indies won by 32 runs.
West Indies 244-7 (60 ov);
New Zealand 212-9 (60 ov)

Group A: England v Australia
at Lord's – 9 June
England won by 6 wickets.
Australia 159-9 (6 ov);
England 160-4 (47.4 ov)

Group A: Australia v Pakistan
at Nottingham – 13-14 June
Pakistan won by 89 runs.
Pakistan 287-7 (60 ov);
Australia 197 (57.1 ov)

Group A: Australia v Canada
at Birmingham – 16 June
Australia won by 7 wickets.
Canada 105 (33.2 ov);
Australia 106-3 (26 ov)

Group A: Pakistan v Canada
at Leeds – 9 June
Pakistan won by 8 wickets.
Canada 139-9 (60 ov);
Pakistan 140-2 (40.1 ov)

Group A: England v Canada
at Manchester – 13-14 June
England won by 8 wickets.
Canada 45 (40.3 ov);
England 46-2 (13.5 ov)

Group A: England v Pakistan
at Leeds – 16 June
England won by 14 runs.
England 165-9 (60 ov);
Pakistan 151 (56 ov)

The final eight teams in the 1979 World Cup at Lord's; the captains (front row) from left: A P B Tennekoon (Sri Lanka), Asif Iqbal (Pakistan), Clive Lloyd (West Indies), Mike Brearley (England), Kim Hughes (Australia), Mark Burgess (New Zealand) and S Venkataraghavan (India)

Opposite page: England celebrate as Gordon Greenidge is run out at Lord's

SUMMARY OF RESULTS

GROUP A

TEAM	POINTS	PLAYED	WON	LOSS	NO RESULT	RUN RATE
England	12	3	3	0	0	3.07
Pakistan	8	3	2	1	0	3.60
Australia	4	3	1	2	0	3.16
Canada	0	3	0	3	0	1.60

GROUP B

TEAM	POINTS	PLAYED	WON	LOSS	NO RESULT	RUN RATE
West Indies	10	3	2	0	1	3.93
New Zealand	8	3	2	1	0	3.55
Sri Lanka	6	3	1	1	1	3.56
India	0	3	0	3	0	3.13

1ST SEMI-FINAL
England v New Zealand at Manchester – 20 June
England won by 9 runs.
England 221-8 (60 ov);
New Zealand 212-9 (60 ov)

2ND SEMI-FINAL
Pakistan v West Indies at The Oval – 20 June
West Indies won by 43 runs.
West Indies 293-6 (60 ov);
Pakistan 250 (56.2 ov)

FINAL
West Indies v England at Lord's – 23 June
West Indies won by 92 runs.
West Indies 286-9 (60 ov);
England 194 (51 ov)

1983 England

Thousands of fans swarm Lord's after India stun West Indies

No Lording It over India

THE third World Cup, the last to be sponsored by the Prudential Assurance Company, began and ended with India. The underdogs beat West Indies, two-time world champions. Kapil Dev's India arrived in England in 1983, without expectations. In two World Cups they had beaten only East Africa and lost to Sri Lanka, a team yet to be granted Test status. Thus, what unfolded was a magical and memorable journey that culminated in a historic day at Lord's, one that put India on the map and forever changed the course of the 50-over game.

This Prudential Cup, as the previous two, had two groups, but this time each team played the others in its group twice, instead of once, to determine the four semi-finalists. England dominated Group A by twice disposing of Pakistan and Sri Lanka, and were joined in the semi-finals by Pakistan, who barely managed to sneak in owing to a marginally higher run rate than New Zealand.

For the first time, non-Test grounds were used, and it was one such venue, the charming Neville Ground in Tunbridge Wells, which Kapil chose to become the inspiration for India's World Cup success. He got his team firing with a stunning 138-ball unbeaten 175, which included 16 fours and six sixes, against Zimbabwe. The Indians carried that momentum into the semis, making history at Chelmsford, thanks largely to Roger Binny and Madan Lal, who were superb in medium-pace tandem. India then usurped hosts England in the semi-finals, with Mohinder Amarnath turning in a fine all-round display and Yashpal Sharma emerging from relative obscurity with a stylish 61. They followed that by defeating West Indies, who had brushed aside Australia and Zimbabwe in the league and Pakistan in the semis.

India, with just 17 wins in their first nine years of playing ODI cricket, were considered fortunate to just be at a World Cup final. Taking on the mighty West Indies meant that they were but lambs to the slaughter. When India were reduced to 183, it was all going to script. But then something extraordinary happened. Inspired by an unforgettable running catch by Kapil, India's bowlers turned canny; the fielders, electric; and West Indies, complacent. In a blaze of glory, the rank outsiders had overcome gargantuan odds and stood atop the world.

India's victory remains the biggest upset ever in international cricket, but beyond all the glory that it brought the country, India's success at Lord's made cricket a global sport.

Opposite page: Ian Botham is bowled by the infamous shooter from Kirti Azad in the semis

GROUP A: ENGLAND, PAKISTAN, NEW ZEALAND AND SRI LANKA

GROUP B: WEST INDIES, INDIA, AUSTRALIA AND ZIMBABWE

1983 Prudential World Cup statistics

Formats Round robin and Knockout

Host England

Champions India (first title)

Participants 8

Matches played 27

Attendance 232,081 (8,596 per match)

Most runs David Gower (384)

Most wickets Roger Binny (18)

Roger Binny became the highest wicket-taker in a World Cup with 18 victims.

1983

Bob Willis had figures of 9-4-9-1 in England's nine wicket thrashing of Sri Lanka at Headingley.

Zimbabwe captain Fletcher is the Man of the Match after his team stuns Australia

Australia v Zimbabwe
9 June
Third match, Nottingham

ZIMBABWE started their World Cup sojourn in the most incredible manner, beating Australia by 13 runs in the tournament opener at Trent Bridge. Their captain, Duncan Fletcher, walked to the middle when Zimbabwe's innings were on the verge of collapse and hit a cool 69 to set up a fighting total. Australia were cruising along at 61 for no loss in reply, but Fletcher returned, snapped up four vital Australian top-order wickets that set up the historic triumph. *The Times* noted that 'few more deserving victories have been obtained'.

India v West Indies
9-10 June
Fourth match, Manchester

THERE was another upset on the opening day of the Prudential Cup. At Old Trafford, India – who had won only one previous Prudential Cup match, against East Africa in 1975 – downed West Indies. From 79 for 3 in 22 overs, India posted their highest score in three World Cups, thanks to Yashpal Sharma's 89. Their bowlers backed up that effort with a canny display that saw West Indies slip from 67 for 2 in 22 overs to 157 for 9 in the 47th over. A last-wicket stand of 71 between Andy Roberts and Joel Garner gave India a fright, but a smart stumping by Syed Kirmani brought them victory.

England v Sri Lanka
11 June
Fifth match, Taunton

DAVID GOWER was cut off on 39 in his first innings of the tournament, but up against Sri Lanka on a good batting deck he stroked his way to 130, complete with five sixes and 12 fours. Gower went on to become the highest run-getter of the Prudential World Cup (384 runs from seven matches), and this was his showpiece innings. England stuttered with the run-outs of Mike Gatting and Ian Botham, but the blue-eyed, curly-haired Gower drove and cut fluently to set up a winning total. Though batting with spirit, Sri Lanka were never in sight of making the 334 they needed.

Australia v West Indies
11-12 June
Seventh match, Leeds

IF Kapil Dev's 175 was the batting master-class of the round, the stellar bowling performance came from West Indies' Winston Davis, who demolished Australia at Headingley with a World-Cup-record 7 for 51. David was a rookie in the side and was drafted in for this match after West Indies were upset by India in their opening encounter. On a tough surface, West Indies were defending 252 in a match that crossed over into the second day because of inclement weather. Australia had recovered from an ugly blow to Graeme Wood that sent him to hospital with concussion, when Davis entered the fray. His first wicket, Kim Hughes caught by Clive Lloyd, was followed by a return to snap a threatening stand of 59, and that kick-started a spell that blew the

Martin Snedden conceded the most runs in an ODI - 2 for 105 off 12 overs against England.

Aussies away. Davis took six of the last seven wickets, at a personal cost of 14 runs. It was, by all accounts, an astonishing display of fast bowling.

Winston Davis was devastating against Australia at Headingley

India v Zimbabwe

18 June

Twentieth match, Tunbridge Wells

THE definitive innings of the 1983 World Cup was played amid the non-descript surroundings of the Neville Ground in quaint Tunbridge Wells. Alas, the BBC was on strike, and there were no cameras present at the ground on this balmy summer afternoon. Never mind that it came against World Cup debutants Zimbabwe, this century stands the test of time for it was at 9 for 4 that Kapil walked to the middle and etched his name in the game's history. The score became 17 for 5 but Kapil batted on a different level. He was composed and elegant, brutal yet majestic. By the time he was done, India had 266 for 8. Single-handedly, Kapil scripted the definitive Indian one-day innings, showing a nerve that his team-mates would look back on for inspiration as the World Cup proceeded. He received significant support from Syed Kirmani, who made an unbeaten 24 in a record ninth-wicket stand. Once he reached his century in the 49th over, Kapil exploded – 75 runs flew from his bat in the next 11 overs.

India v West Indies

20 June

Twenty-third match, Chelmsford

THIS was an epic match in the context of India's World Cup dream. Had they lost to Australia here, they would have been ousted on the basis of Australia's better head-to-head record, and so the match at Chelmsford was one of life and death. Coming to this match, Australia weren't in the best of shape, with their bowling especially suspect, but on this day, they managed to bowl India out for 247 in 55.5 overs. From a poor start (3 for 1), Australia were looking good on 46 for 1 when Roger Binny, in his most outstanding display of an outstanding World Cup, knocked the stuffing out of them. In three overs, the 16th, the 18th and the 20th, Binny reduced the Aussies to 52 for 4, and the game was over as a contest. Bowling seam-up and hitting all the right places, Binny confounded the opposition with just the right pace on that wicket, and claimed match-winning figures of 8-2-29-4. In many ways, Binny was the epitome of India's spirit that summer, and it was here, at Chelmsford, that his indefatigable spirit was on display.

Kapil Dev holds aloft the 1983 World Cup trophy

1983

There were over twice as many wides per match in 1983 as compared to 1979 (9.59 to 4.64).

England v India
22 June, First semi-final, Manchester

TWO moments really stood out in this match: Yashpal Sharma hitting Bob Willis for six and Kirti Azad bowling Ian Botham with a shooter that rolled along the turf. On both occasions, an obscure Indian had humbled a famous Englishman. Azad was an innocuous offspinner who had his day when he helped bottle up the middle order with his fastish offbreaks, and earned a bonus while bowling the dangerous Botham. Later, during India's chase, Yashpal contemptuously flicked Willis for six during a crucial third-wicket stand with Mohinder Amarnath. That, like Azad's shooter, was to become part of the indelible memory of India's glory run.

Pakistan v West Indies
22 June, Second semi-final, The Oval, London

THE two teams met again in the semis and, once again, West Indies won, though this was far from a high-scoring affair. Pakistan were a highly talented team, under the astute captaincy of Imran Khan, and had played well in the group stage. But without Javed Miandad, who was down with influenza, the batsmen struggled on a good surface, and a huffing-and-puffing innings ended at 184 for 6. Mohsin Khan's 76 was the best score, but his strike-rate of 36.77 told a different story. Malcolm Marshall and Michael Holding shared five wickets and never allowed the Pakistanis to dominate. Neither Gordon Greenidge nor Desmond Haynes was able to provide a breathtaking assault, but that was made up for with an unbeaten stand of 132 between Viv Richards and Larry Gomes as West Indies stormed into their third successive World Cup final with 11.2 overs to spare. The signs were ominous for India, even though they were the only team to have beaten West Indies in the tournament.

Opposite page: The rhododendrons were in bloom as Kapil Dev smashed 175 against Zimbabwe

THE FINALS India v West Indies **25 June, Lord's, London**

A total of 232,081 fans strolled in to Lord's on this sunny day, nearly equalling the combined total of past two finals (160,000 for 1975 & 132,000 for 1979). Clive Lloyd won the toss and West Indies were briefly held by Kris Srikanth who cut, pulled and drove his way to 38 from 57 balls, but from 90 for 2 India combusted. Once Srikanth and Mohinder Amarnath, whose sheet anchor 26 would prove to be invaluable, were separated Yashpal Sharma's fine tournament ended in failure, and Kapil Dev, Kirti Azad and Roger Binny all stumbled. Sandeep Patil and the lower order rallied to get the total to 183, crucially ensuring India batted for 54.4 overs.

Balwinder Sandhu took new ball and gave India an immense breakthrough, foxing Gorden Greenidge with an inswinger that hit the West Indies opener on the fingers and crashed onto stumps. It was the first of two pivotal moments. The second, Kapil's running catch to dismiss Viv Richards, was the turning point.

Three wickets left the Caribbean giants 66 for 4, and when a hobbling Lloyd drove Madan Lal to Kapil in the covers, the score was 66 for 5. It got worse at 76 for 6, but a stubborn rear-guard effort between Jeff Dujon and Malcolm Marshall threatened to undo all the good work. Then Kapil called Amarnath into the attack and, in typically languid style, he removed the pair to leave West Indies at 124 for 8. Jogging, hiding the ball behind his back, hitting the seam and extracting extra bounce, Amarnath stunned the defending champions. The final nail was hammered when he trapped Michael Holding lbw, a scene that was captured on television and photographs for all Indian fans to cherish forever.

Pakistan hit only two fours in their 184 for 8 off 60 overs against West Indies in the semi-finals.

Sunil Walson, who was part of the 1983 World Cup winning team, never played for India in ODIs.

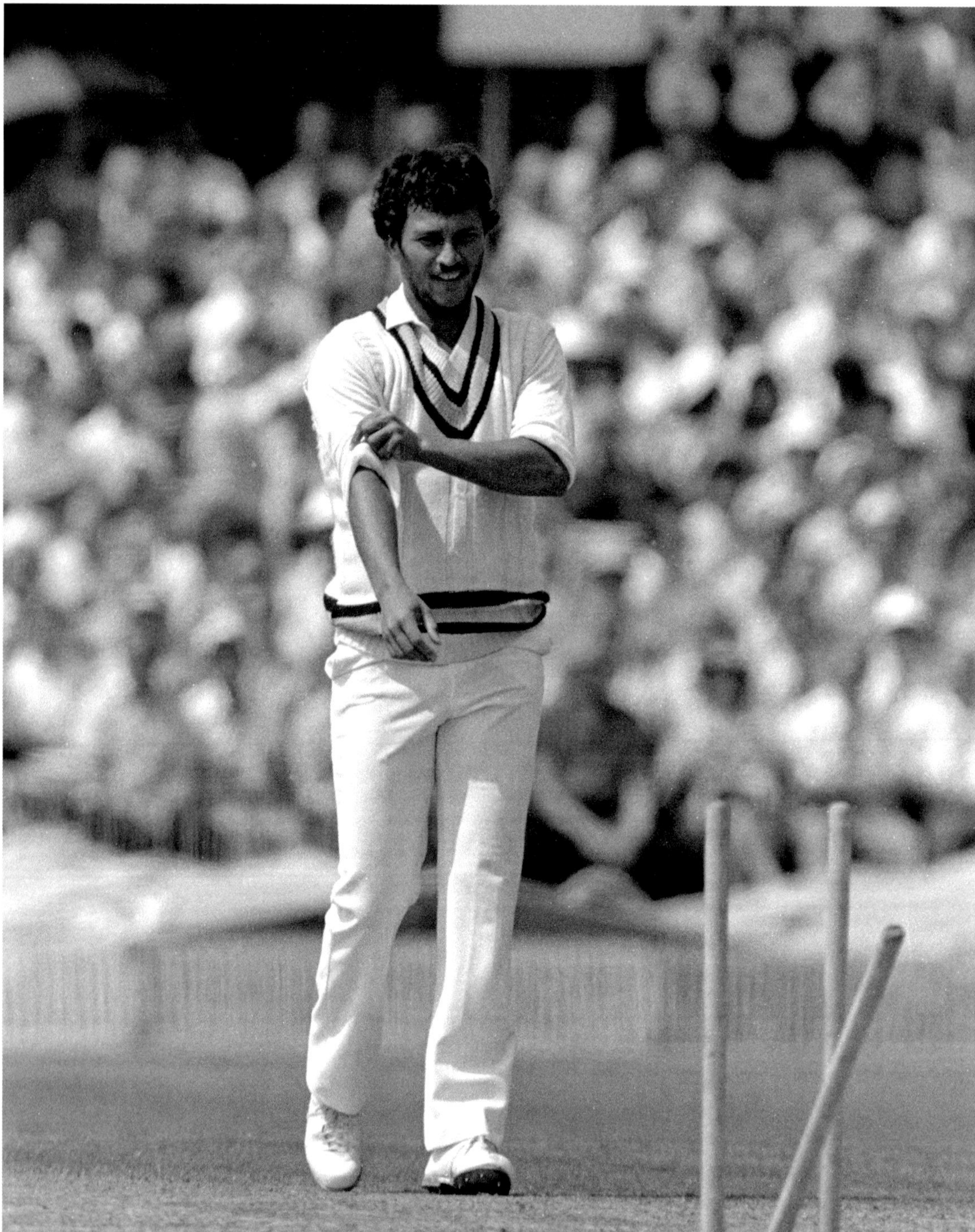

An Indian summer

Roger Binny
World Cup winner and highest wicket-taker of the tournament

THE Indian public and media weren't that confident of our abilities in England that summer, despite our success in the West Indies earlier that year, but the mood within the team was upbeat. This tour was far more significant than people probably realized at the time. India lost the Tests and the one-day series against a West Indies side at their peak, but a lot of positives were derived from that series. There was one particular match, in Berbice [where India defended a total of 282 for 5 in 47 overs, with Kapil Dev hitting 72 and claiming 2 for 33], and the success there acted as a catalyst of sorts when we landed in England.

The Berbice victory came up for discussion just before our first match, against West Indies at Manchester. We spoke of the significance of that match, and how it was the first time we had beaten West Indies. A lot of the boys took inspiration from that match and we said 'look, we've done it once, why not again?'. And that was that. We went on to beat West Indies in the first match of the World Cup and that was a massive confidence-booster. It really was surreal, as I recall it.

Personally, I had had a good Ranji Trophy season and was feeling good about the tournament. Then I started to get wickets, and we did well. But I must say that never did we get overconfident. After we beat Zimbabwe the first time, the defeat to Australia at Nottingham was , in a way, good for us because it kept us grounded. It also made us hungry for more.

West Indies had their revenge [at The Oval] and then we came up against Zimbabwe on what was a tricky wicket at Tunbridge Wells. I don't think much needs to be said about what happened here. Kapil's innings was simply outstanding, and this was a huge moment for us, statistically and psychologically. If I recall correctly, he didn't' hit a six until he had crossed 100, after which he opened up and stunned Zimbabwe.

Personally, the second match against Australia at Chelmsford was very satisfying. I was in the wickets, and this just happened to be a great day for me. There was a lot of pressure on us, because had we lost to Australia it was all over. We had to win, and again it was Yashpal and Sandeep Patil who batted very well to get us to a good score. Then Madan Lal and I found a good rhythm and managed to bowl them out for not much [129 in 38.2 overs].

The semi-final against England was immense. Once again, Yashpal was at his best and Sandeep just batted beautifully. The way they chased down England's total was superb.

Then, of course, the final: to beat West Indies, that West Indies team, at Lords – unbelievable. The turning points were [Balwinder] Sandhu bowling Gordon Greenidge and then Kapil's catch to dismissed [Viv] Richards. What a catch! That day we showed the world that we belonged.

Another aspect of that summer I can never forget is the support we received from Indians, those who were living in England and who had followed us from home. Everywhere we went, they thronged to the grounds and carried with them food and flowers; many even invited us into their homes. We had some vegetarians in the team – Kris Srikanth, Yashpal, to name a few – and finding vegetarian food in England was at times difficult. But the fans always turned up with something that we could all eat. It was such a sense of support for us, and I think we repaid them by winning the World Cup.

Opposite page: Roger Binny's best display of the World Cup came against Australia in a do-or-die match

SUMMARY OF RESULTS

GROUP STAGE

Group A: England v New Zealand
at The Oval – 9 June
England won by 106 runs.
England 322-6 (60 ov);
New Zealand 216 (59 ov)

Group A: Pakistan v Sri Lanka
at Swansea – 9 June
Pakistan won by 50 runs.
Pakistan 338-5 (60 ov);
Sri Lanka 288-9 (60 ov)

Group B: Australia v Zimbabwe
at Nottingham – 9 June
Zimbabwe won by 13 runs.
Zimbabwe 239-6 (60 ov);
Australia 226-7 (60 ov)

Group B: India v West Indies
at Manchester – 9 June
India won by 34 runs.
India 262-8 (60 ov);
West Indies 228 (54.1 ov)

Group A: England v Sri Lanka
at Taunton – 11 June
England won by 47 runs.
England 333-9 (60 ov);
Sri Lanka 286 (58 ov)

Group A: New Zealand v Pakistan
at Birmingham – 11 June
New Zealand won by 52 runs.
New Zealand 238-9 (60 ov);
Pakistan 186 (55.2 ov)

Group B: Australia v West Indies
at Leeds – 11 June
West Indies won by 101 runs.
West Indies 252-9 (60 ov);
Australia 151 (30.3 ov)

Group B: India v Zimbabwe
at Leicester – 11 June
India won by 5 wickets.
Zimbabwe 155 (51.4 ov);
India 157-5 (37.3 ov)

Group A: England v Pakistan
at Lord's – 13 June
England won by 8 wickets.
Pakistan 193-8 (60 ov);
England 199-2 (50.4 ov)

Group A: New Zealand v Sri Lanka
at Bristol – 13 June
New Zealand won by 5 wickets.
Sri Lanka 206 (56.1 ov);
New Zealand 209-5 (39.2 ov)

Group B: Australia v India
at Nottingham – 13 June
Australia won by 162 runs.
Australia 320-9 (60 ov);
India 158 (37.5 ov)

Group B: West Indies v Zimbabwe
at Worcester – 13 June
West Indies won by 8 wickets.
Zimbabwe 217-7 (60 ov);
West Indies 218-2 (48.3 ov)

Group A: England v New Zealand
at Birmingham – 15 June
New Zealand won by 2 wickets.
England 234 (55.2 ov);
New Zealand 238-8 (59.5 ov)

Group B: India v West Indies
at The Oval – 15 June
West Indies won by 66 runs.
West Indies 282-9 (60 ov);
India 216 (53.1 ov)

Group A: Pakistan v Sri Lanka
at Leeds – 16 June
Pakistan won by 11 runs.
Pakistan 235-7 (60 ov);
Sri Lanka 224 (58.3 ov)

Group B: Australia v Zimbabwe
at Southampton – 16 June
Australia won by 32 runs.
Australia 272-7 (60 ov);
Zimbabwe 240 (59.5 ov)

Group A: England v Pakistan
at Manchester – 18 June
England won by 7 wickets.
Pakistan 232-8 (60 ov);
England 233-3 (57.2 ov)

Group A: New Zealand v Sri Lanka
at Derby – 18 June
Sri Lanka won by 3 wickets.
New Zealand 181 (58.2 ov);
Sri Lanka 184-7 (52.5 ov)

Group B: Australia v West Indies
at Lord's – 18 June
West Indies won by 7 wickets.
Australia 273-6 (60 ov);
West Indies 276-3 (57.5 ov)

Group B: India v Zimbabwe
at Tunbridge Wells – 18 June
India won by 31 runs.
India 266-8 (60 ov);
Zimbabwe 235 (57 ov)

Group A: England v Sri Lanka
at Leeds – 20 June
England won by 9 wickets.
Sri Lanka 136 (50.4 ov);
England 137-1 (24.1 ov)

Group A: New Zealand v Pakistan
at Nottingham – 20 June
Pakistan won by 11 runs.
Pakistan 261-3 (60 ov);
New Zealand 250 (59.1 ov)

Group B: Australia v India
at Chelmsford – 20 June
India won by 118 runs.
India 247 (55.5 ov);
Australia 129 (38.2 ov)

Group B: West Indies v Zimbabwe
at Birmingham – 20 June
West Indies won by 10 wickets.
Zimbabwe 171 (60 ov);
West Indies 172-0 (45.1 ov)

SUMMARY OF RESULTS

GROUP A						
TEAM	POINTS	PLAYED	WON	LOSS	NO RESULT	RUN RATE
England	20	6	5	1	0	4.671
Pakistan	12	6	3	3	0	4.014
New Zealand	12	6	3	3	0	3.927
Sri Lanka	4	6	1	5	0	3.752

GROUP B						
TEAM	POINTS	PLAYED	WON	LOSS	NO RESULT	RUN RATE
West Indies	20	6	5	1	0	4.308
India	16	6	4	2	0	3.870
Australia	8	6	2	4	0	3.808
Zimbabwe	4	6	1	5	0	3.492

Kris Srikkanth square-drives Andy Roberts at Lord's

1ST SEMI-FINAL

England v India at Manchester – 22 June
India won by 6 wickets.
England 213 (60 ov);
India 217-4 (54.4 ov)

2ND SEMI-FINAL

Pakistan v West Indies at The Oval – 22 June
West Indies won by 8 wickets.
Pakistan 184-8 (60 ov);
West Indies 188-2 (48.4 ov)

FINAL

India v West Indies at Lord's – 25 June
India won by 43 runs.
India 183 (54.4 ov);
West Indies 140 (52 ov)

1987 India & Pakistan

Allan Border's Australia pose with the trophy after beating England at Eden Gardens

Border's Skirmish

INDIA'S success in 1983 prompted the country's administrators to bid for staging rights for the 1987 World Cup, which marked the first significant shift in the balance of power in international cricket.

Even though neither India nor Pakistan made it to the final, the Reliance Cup drew more eyeballs, was more tensely contested, and was by far a more vibrant affair than its three predecessors held in England. It was a huge success in terms of cricketing revenue and media coverage, and brought the Indian subcontinent under the limelight as one of the prospective homes of cricket. Title sponsor Reliance pumped in ₹ 2.2 crore, and each Test-playing nation received guarantee money of £200,000, while qualifiers Zimbabwe collected £170,000.

Viv Richards, writing in *Sportsweek*, deemed the tournament a success: 'The Reliance Cup was a wonderful experience....I think the Reliance Cup effectively quashed the belief that a tournament of this nature could be stage-managed in one country only.'

This time around, owing to shorter daylight hours in the subcontinent, games were 50 overs per innings, not 60. This was also the first time that neutral umpires were appointed. At 21 venues, India hosted 17 matches, including a semi-final and the final; while Pakistan hosted 10 matches. India were expected to go far, given their success in Australia in 1985, but having qualified by playing in a weaker group, they struggled against tougher sides. Pakistan, co-hosts, bolted out of the stables and won their first give matches, thanks largely to Imran Khan and Abdul Qadir, only to fall apart in the semi-finals.

West Indies and New Zealand were recovering from the absence of their strike bowlers, yet made themselves heard intermittently. Sri Lanka were still something of a fledgling team and appeared overawed by the occasion, while Zimbabwe appeared naïve, even if their fielding drew applause. England somehow managed to overcome the heat and food, thanks to a big-hearted bowling attack, but lost the plot in the final against an unfancied Australian team that – through sheer energy and perseverance and the consistent David Boon (447 runs at 55.87), Geoff Marsh (428 at 61.14), and Craig McDermott (18 wickets at 18.94) – trumped the odds.

The Australian team that arrived in India looked different from the side that had surrendered the Ashes nine months ago. Marsh and Boon gave Australia a tremendous start, Dean Jones was consistent thereafter; Steve Waugh and Mike Veletta could score quickly in the middle, and this masked over the limited success of Border the batsman. In purely sporting parameters, the Reliance Cup of 1987 was more pivotal than the 1983 World Cup.

Opposite page: Graham Gooch swept India out of the 1987 World Cup with a gritty innings in the semis

GROUP A: AUSTRALIA, INDIA, NEW ZEALAND AND ZIMBABWE

GROUP B: WEST INDIES, PAKISTAN, SRI LANKA AND ENGLAND

1987 Reliance World Cup statistics

Formats Round robin and Knockout

Host India and Pakistan

Champions Australia (first title)

Participants 8

Matches played 27

Most runs Graham Gooch (471)

Most wickets Craig McDermott (18)

Craig McDermott was the bowling hero of the Reliance World Cup with 18 at 18.94.

Imran Khan, with 17 wickets, enjoyed the best bowling average of the tournament: 13.05.

England's Paul Downton leaps for the ball during a World Cup match at Gujranwala

England v West Indies

9 October

Second match, Gujranwala

THE tournament was given an early spark when England succeeded in scoring 35 off their last three overs to beat West Indies. England looked down and out when they required 91 from the final 10 overs with four wickets in hand, but Allan Lamb changed gears in the company of John Emburey and Phil DeFreitas. England's target was 35 from three overs, but Lamb looted 15 from a 19-run Courtney Walsh over. Patrick Patterson gave just six from the penultimate over, meaning the target for England was 13 from six. Lamb began with a couple and a four off the hapless Walsh, who then sprayed four wides down the leg side and followed up with a no-ball, from which Lamb scampered a single. The next ball was a deplorable full toss, which Neil Foster put away for four to seal a thriller.

India v Australia

9 October

Third match, Madras

ANY doubts about the tournament were put to rest when India, defending champions, were beaten by Australia by one run. A little over a year after the famous tied Test in Madras, the same teams played out a lesser classic – though an equally tight ODI – at the same venue. India, with eight wickets in hand, needed roughly 70 off the last 15 overs. Craig McDermott, who had bled 31 from his first four overs, came back to take out the middle order. Still, India needed only 15 from four overs with four wickets remaining. Somehow, they contrived to leave themselves eight to get from the final over, with the last

Navjot Singh Sidhu's first four innings of the Reliance World Cup were: 73, 75, 51 and 55.

man, Maninder Singh, to face Steve Waugh. Kiran More ran himself out, Maninder pinched two doubles, but he was bowled on the final ball with India two runs short. In the end, a call taken earlier in the day proved heart-breaking: one of Dean Jones's two sixes had been signalled as four by the match referee Intikhab Alam; but during the innings break, Kapil Dev sportingly concurred with Australia's insistence that the ball had crossed the ropes. Thus India's target was increased by two runs. Australia were no strangers to close matches, and this game demonstrated that they were able to hold their nerve in tight situations. That victory was a sign of things to come; Australia eventually won the tournament by beating England by a mere seven runs in the final.

New Zealand v Zimbabwe

10 October

Fourth match, Hyderabad

FOR sheer heroism, the best innings of the World Cup was David Houghton's 142 against New Zealand. Houghton, Zimbabwe's wicketkeeper-batsman, nearly took his team to a memorable win, single-handedly. Chasing 243, Zimbabwe had slipped to 104 for 7 before Houghton added 117 with Iain Butchard – an ODI record for the eighth wicket – and had taken them to within 22 runs of victory when he was dismissed in the 47th over. His outstanding innings of 142 spanned 138 balls and consisted of three sixes and 13 fours. Zimbabwe didn't win in 1987, but Houghton's heroics helped them return home with their egos intact.

Sri Lanka v West Indies

13 October

Seventh match, Karachi

VIV RICHARDS' 181 in only 125 deliveries against Sri Lanka stood as a tournament record for 12 years. West Indies had gotten off to a shaky start in the Reliance Cup, and when they came up against Sri Lanka in Karachi, it was a side itching to dominate. Matters began horribly, however, and Richards strode out needing to avert a hat-trick. He did so easily, and appeared intent on playing a long innings, reaching his fifty off 62 balls. Then, in true marauding manner, the master blaster larruped 81 from the next 33 balls to completely shut out Sri Lanka. His 10th one-day international century, unprecedented at the time, took just 97 balls. Partnering Richards was the centurion Desmond Haynes, but few remember that. The pair shared a 182-run stand in 177 balls, with Richards smacking six sixes and 16 fours in a blazing innings that spanned just 125 balls. West Indies finished on 360 for 4, the highest score in a World Cup game till Sri Lanka themselves eclipsed it nine years later.

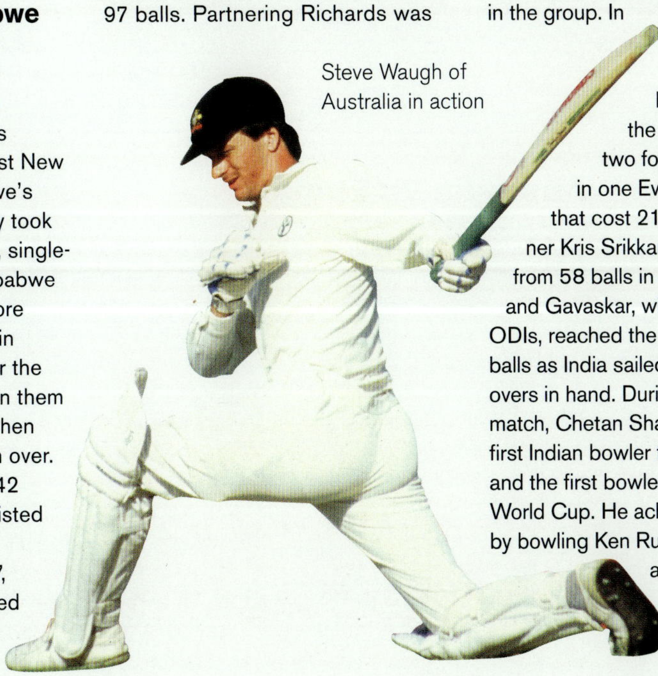

Steve Waugh of Australia in action

India v New Zealand

31 October

Twenty-fourth match, Nagpur

WITH his career winding down, Sunil Gavaskar played the sort of innings few expected from him. Averaging 50 in the tournament, Gavaskar scored his first and only ODI century in Nagpur. India needed to score 222 from 42.2 overs to beat New Zealand and claim top sport ahead of Australia in the group. In 1987, chasing 5.25 an over was quite something, but Gavaskar set the tone by taking two fours and two sixes in one Ewan Chatfield over that cost 21. His opening partner Kris Srikkanth slammed 75 from 58 balls in a century stand and Gavaskar, with 105 previous ODIs, reached the landmark in 85 balls as India sailed home with 10 overs in hand. During that same match, Chetan Sharma became the first Indian bowler to claim a hat-trick, and the first bowler to ever do so in a World Cup. He achieved the landmark by bowling Ken Rutherford, Ian Smith and Chatfield with the last three balls of the 42nd over.

Courtney Walsh's decision not to run out the last Pakistani batsman cost West Indies the World Cup.

THE SEMI-FINALS

Pakistan v Australia

4 November, First semi-final, Lahore

IN the build-up to this match, Allan Border's Australia had been termed a bunch of club cricketers by Zaheer Abbas. A determined bunch of scrappers needed no further incentive to lift their game and rub it in Pakistan's face. Despite a three-wicket burst from Imran Khan, Australia finished on 267 as Steve Waugh took 18 off the final over bowled by Salim Jaffer. Craig McDermott had been crucial in getting Australia this far, and he began his spell by bowling Mansoor Akhtar. Pakistan, though, were being revived from 38 for 3 by Imran Khan and Javed Miandad. Once they were separated, Pakistan folded to McDermott, who bowled Wasim Akram and got Salim Yousuf, Jaffer and Tauseef Ahmed to nick to the wicketkeeper. Australia won, and McDermott finished with 5 for 54, the best figures of the tournament. As Border said after Australia's 18-run victory: 'When Zaheer Abbas called us a bunch of club cricketers, I knew we would be sparking today. Our boys take a fancy to that sort of talk.'

India v England

5 November, Second semi-final, Bombay

INDIA qualified for the semis on the back of Gavaskar's swan song and Sharma's hat-tricks, but when they reached Bombay, they contrived to stumble. After Kapil Dev asked England to bat on a tricky surface, Graham Gooch and Mike Gatting got down and dirtied and swept and pulled themselves a 117-run alliance in 19 overs. That paved the way for a total of 254, which proved too much for India's vaunted batting line-up, missing Dilip Vengsarkar with a stomach bug. Kris Srikkanth and Navjot Singh Sidhu, dashers alike, weren't able to pinch a single boundary and the pressure built up. Eddy Hemmings ended the match with 4 for 21 in 34 balls and England, through sheer commitment, dashed the host's aspirations of a place in the final.

Opposite page: England's Bill Athey is run out against Australia during the final

THE FINALS Australia Vs England 8 November, Calcutta

ONCE again opting to bat, Australia put up the highest score in a World Cup final and that was enough to give Allan Border and his band of merry men immense confidence when they took the field to defend 253. But it wasn't so easy. Having helped sweep, literally, India out of the World Cup a few days earlier, Mike Gatting chose the final of the Reliance Cup to try out a very risky shot. It would prove the decisive play of the match. In front of 100,000 fans, most of who were backing them, England were well-placed in their pursuit of 254 at 135 for 2, with captain Gatting and Bill Athey at the crease. Enter Border for some part-time left-arm spin. He tossed the ball up on around off stump; Gatting got down on his haunches, and out came the reverse-sweep. But it was not executed well at all; the ball flew off the shoulder of the bat and straight to Greg Dyer. One moment of madness brought Australia back into the game, and when the dangerous Phil DeFreitas was brilliantly held by Bruce Reid on the boundary, Australia knew they had won. Once again, England were beaten in a World Cup final. The Australians hosted their leader on their shoulders, World Cup in hand, and did a lap of honour that was wholeheartedly cheered by the fans. Fireworks were going off in the stands and, as a few players would later admit, it was like a scene out of a movie.

Jeff Crowe captained New Zealand in a solitary Test before being handed the leadership in 1987.

1987

'To lose patience is to lose the battle'

Geoff Marsh

1987 World Cup winner and third-highest run-scorer of the tournament

Australian cricket had had its share of turbulence in the years between the previous World Cup and the one we set out to compete in, largely because we had lost the Ashes at home in 1986, and there wasn't a whole lot of excitement about our departure or chances at the 1987 tournament. But people seemed to forget that we'd played some very good cricket, albeit in patches, in the build-up to 1987.

We had come over to India the previous year for a full tour, and so we knew what we were up against in terms of the heat, conditions and extensive travel. I think that was a big advantage we had as compared to some of the other overseas teams.

I remember landing in Mumbai and during the drive from the airport to the team hotel, Simon O'Donnell looked out the window and pointed to an advertising banner that said: 'To lose patience is to lose the battle'. None of us forgot that and we used that as a rallying charge throughout the tournament.

That first match against India, where we won by such a slim margin, was just what we needed. It again showed that we could win in adversity. From there we got some momentum going, helped by the fact that we won the toss and batted in five of six qualifying games. Our batsmen were in form – David Boon and I were able to provide good starts – and the bowlers backed us up really well. Each department complimented each other, but I'd say it was our fielding that set us apart.

We also had the best coach in the world, Bob Simpson, and he made us work very, very hard. Simpson's contribution to our win is under-rated; he was a driving force and together with our captain, Allan Border, really pushed us to excel.

My partnerships with Boon were memorable, personally. We went way back, to our Under-16 playing days, and we'd come up together. We fed off each other at the crease and had a smooth understanding of the way we batted. That worked really well for us in 1987.

I remember the semi-final against Pakistan, and how the comments made by Zaheer Abbas riled up AB. We went out there charged up, put runs on the board, and then Craig McDermott bowled the spell of the tournament. That win gave us tremendous satisfaction and we marched into the final.

The final was tremendous, in terms of the atmosphere at Eden Gardens and the way the full house backed us. Obviously, Mike Gatting's reverse-sweep remains a talking point and, yes, it was the turning point. He'd been caught on the ropes earlier in the innings by Steve Waugh but his foot fell onto the rope. I guess pressure took its toll on Gatting, who was dead keen to play the sweep. But the reverse-sweep was a high percentage shot and on that day it didn't pay off. We didn't let up after that.

Beating England was amazing, but what gave me the greatest pleasure was how we had come to India so determined to win and that we had managed to sustain that level of performance all through. We won two very close matches – against India and New Zealand. India should have won that match, but we did. Same against New Zealand. Winning two matches when you really shouldn't have is a different kind of inspiration. We never let ourselves get down and that banner we'd seen on the team bus remained our inspiration all tournament.

Opposite page: Geoff Marsh's batting was extremely crucial for Australia's success in India

SUMMARY OF RESULTS

GROUP STAGE

Group B: Pakistan v Sri Lanka
at Hyderabad – 8 October
Pakistan won by 15 runs.
Pakistan 267-6 (50 ov);
Sri Lanka 252 (49.2 ov)

Group A: India v Australia
at Chennai – 9 October
Australia won by 1 run.
Australia 270-6 (50 ov);
India 269 (49.5 ov)

Group B: England v West Indies
at Gujranwala – 9 October
England won by 2 wickets.
West Indies 243-7 (50 ov);
England 246-8 (49.3 ov)

Group A: New Zealand v Zimbabwe
at Hyderabad – 10 October
New Zealand won by 3 runs.
New Zealand 242-7 (50 ov);
Zimbabwe 239 (49.4 ov)

Group B: Pakistan v England
at Rawalpindi – 12 October
Pakistan won by 18 runs.
Pakistan 239-7 (50 ov);
England 221 (48.4 ov)

Group A: Australia v Zimbabwe
at Chennai – 13 October
Australia won by 96 runs.
Australia 235-9 (50 ov);
Zimbabwe 139 (42.4 ov)

Group B: Sri Lanka v West Indies
at Karachi – 13 October
West Indies won by 191 runs.
West Indies 360-4 (50 ov);
Sri Lanka 169-4 (50 ov)

Group A: India v New Zealand
at Bangalore – 14 October
India won by 16 runs.
India 252-7 (50 ov);
New Zealand 236-8 (50 ov)

Group B: Pakistan v West Indies
at Lahore – 16 October
Pakistan won by 1 wicket.
West Indies 216 (49.3 ov);
Pakistan 217-9 (50 ov)

Group A: India v Zimbabwe
at Mumbai – 17 October
India won by 8 wickets.
Zimbabwe 135 (44.2 ov);
India 136-2 (27.5 ov)

Group B: England v Sri Lanka
at Peshawar – 17 October
England won on faster scoring rate.
England 296-4 (50 ov);
Sri Lanka 158-8 (45 ov)

Group A: Australia v New Zealand
at Indore – 18 October
Australia won by 3 runs.
Australia 199-4 (30 ov);
New Zealand 196-9 (30 ov)

Group B: Pakistan v England
at Karachi – 20 October
Pakistan won by 7 wickets.
England 244-9 (50 ov);
Pakistan 247-3 (49 ov)

Group B: Sri Lanka v West Indies
at Kanpur – 21 October
West Indies won by 25 runs.
West Indies 236-8 (50 ov);
Sri Lanka 211-8 (50 ov)

Group A: India v Australia
at Delhi – 22 October
India won by 56 runs.
India 289-6 (50 ov);
Australia 233 (49 ov)

Group A: New Zealand v Zimbabwe
at Calcutta – 23 October
New Zealand won by 4 wickets.
Zimbabwe 227-5 (50 ov);
New Zealand 228-6 (47.4 ov)

Group B: Pakistan v Sri Lanka
at Faisalabad – 25 October
Pakistan won by 113 runs.
Pakistan 297-7 (50 ov);
Sri Lanka 184-8 (50 ov)

Group A: India v Zimbabwe
at Ahmedabad – 26 October
India won by 7 wickets.
Zimbabwe 191-7 (50 ov);
India 194-3 (42 ov)

Group B: England v West Indies
at Jaipur – 26 October
England won by 34 runs.
England 269-5 (50 ov);
West Indies 235 (48.1 ov)

Group A: Australia v New Zealand
at Chandigarh – 27 October
Australia won by 17 runs.
Australia 251-8 (50 ov);
New Zealand 234 (48.4 ov)

Group A: Australia v Zimbabwe
at Cuttack – 30 October
Australia won by 70 runs.
Australia 266-5 (50 ov);
Zimbabwe 196-6 (50 ov)

Group B: England v Sri Lanka
at Poona – 30 October
England won by 8 wickets.
Sri Lanka 218-7 (50 ov);
England 219-2 (41.2 ov)

Group B: Pakistan v West Indies
at Karachi – 30 October
West Indies won by 28 runs.
West Indies 258-7 (50 ov);
Pakistan 230-9 (50 ov)

Group A: India v New Zealand
at Nagpur – 31 October
India won by 9 wickets.
New Zealand 221-9 (50 ov);
India 224-1 (32.1 ov)

SUMMARY OF RESULTS

GROUP A						
TEAM	POINTS	PLAYED	WON	LOSS	NO RESULT	RUN RATE
India	20	6	5	1	0	5.41
Australia	20	6	5	1	0	5.19
New Zealand	8	6	2	4	0	4.89
Zimbabwe	0	6	0	6	0	3.76

GROUP B						
TEAM	POINTS	PLAYED	WON	LOSS	NO RESULT	RUN RATE
Pakistan	20	6	5	1	0	5.01
England	16	6	4	2	0	5.14
West Indies	12	6	3	3	0	5.16
Sri Lanka	0	6	0	6	0	4.04

Mohammad Azharuddin flicks during the semi-final against England

1ST SEMI-FINAL

Pakistan v Australia at Lahore – 4 November
Australia won by 18 runs.
Australia 267-8 (50 ov);
Pakistan 249 (49 ov)

2ND SEMI-FINAL

India v England at Mumbai – 5 November
England won by 35 runs.
England 254-6 (50 ov);
India 219 (45.3 ov)

FINAL

Australia v England at Calcutta – 8 November
Australia won by 7 runs.
Australia 253-5 (50 ov);
England 246-8 (50 ov)

CIC Insurance
HOOVER

1992 Australia & New Zealand

A packed Sydney Cricket Ground hosts an Australia v England match

A Khan Job

AUSTRALIA and New Zealand were co-hosts of the 1992 World Cup, which saw four major innovations: coloured clothing, with names on the back; floodlights for most of the 36 matches; the white ball, which was used from both ends, much to the bowlers' delight, leading to some sustained spells of high-quality swing and seam bowling; and the fielding rule that only two fielders would be allowed outside the infield for the first 15 overs. As a result of the last rule, teams took a leaf from baseball's book and sent in pinch-hitters at the top of an innings to try and exploit the fielding restrictions. Some weren't so successful, such as Ian Botham, but New Zealand's Mark Greatbatch left an indelible mark on the tournament, thundering down the track to the likes of Malcolm Marshall, Curtly Ambrose and Allan Donald, and his success was the impetus for the likes of Sanath Jayasuriya and others, four years later.

The 1992 World Cup included nine teams that squared off against each other in a league format, implying that there were 39 matches in all – as against 27 in the previous edition – in 33 days. Many found this a trifle too long, but there are many more who feel this format was the best of all World Cups for the reason that it gave each team an equal chance. However, the rule for interrupted matches was roundly criticized, and there was no bigger example of the farcical rules than the semi-final between England and South Africa, who were playing their first World Cup following the end of their 21-year apartheid-induced isolation. South Africa made a good fist of their reply to a target of 253 when the rain came, and at that time they needed 22 runs from 13 deliveries, which was a big task, though not impossible. When the rain stopped , they needed an impossible 21 runs off one ball due to the muddled rules. Needless to say, they lost.

The World Cup began with New Zealand taking on Australia at Eden Park. New Zealand's win set a trend for the rest of the preliminary stage, which saw the holders and favourites, Australia, struggle and New Zealand storm into the semi-finals by virtue of having topped the league by three points after winning seven of eight games. The foundation for that win over Australia was a splendid century from Martin Crowe, the Kiwi captain, who would finish as the World Cup's highest run-getter with 456.

It was in front of a record crowd of 87,182 at the Melbourne Cricket Ground that Imran Khan crowned his glorious career by leading Pakistan to victory. He was one of the game's great bowlers, but he was a fine batsman too and it was in this discipline, as well as captaincy, that he excelled in the tournament. He helped fortify a brittle top order and hit 72 in the final against England and it was somehow fitting that Imran should lift the trophy and never play again.

Pakistan's principle acts were Javed Miandad (437 runs at 62.43), Rameez Raja (349 runs at 58.17), Wasim Akram (18 wickets at 18.78) and Mushtaq Ahmed (16 wickets at 19.44).

Opposite page: Imran Khan celebrates the wicket of Richard Illingworth during the final

1992 World Cup statistics

Formats Round robin and Knockout
Host Australia and New Zealand
Champions Pakistan (first title)
Participants 9
Matches played 39
Attendance 6,21,1214
Most runs Martin Crowe (456)
Most wickets Wasim Akram (18)

Coloured clothing was used for the first time in 1992.

David Boon was Australia's wicketkeeper only once, during the match against India in Brisbane.

England fans had much to cheer about during the 1992 World Cup

New Zealand v Australia

22 February

First match, Auckland

NEW ZEALAND'S World Cup campaign began with a blast, and they used that as motivation to sail all the way to the semi-finals. And it was their captain, Martin Crowe, who led the way with his bat and his mind. From 13 for 2, Crowe added 118 in 25 overs with Ken Rutherford. Despite a dodgy knee, Crowe reached three figures with one ball to spare; as revealed later in his autobiography, *Crowe on Crowe*, he felt the game change when he reached his forties: 'The Australians started to bowl shorter. That was the innings that changed the game'. On an Eden Park pitch that would get slower and lower, Crowe's second masterstroke was to toss the new ball to Jeetan Patel, and offspinner, and to then juggle his attack so frequently that Australia never settled. Patel conceded just 19 from his first seven overs and the asking rate crept up; needing 50 from the last five overs, Australia lost their last five wickets for 12 runs in 17 balls, New Zealand won by 37 runs and Crowe was a national hero.

England v Australia

5 March

Eighteenth match, Sydney

AGING and overweight, Ian Botham cut a poor figure of the hero who wowed England fans for much of the 1980s. By 1992, his portly frame and a failed attempt at theatre back home had got Beefy much criticism, but he still had enough gas in the tank for one final hurrah. Australia, having lost to New Zealand and South Africa, were on the verge of a premature

Ian Botham faced Sachin Tendulkar for the only time in an international match at Perth.

Hansie Cronje of South Africa survives a run-out attempt by Pakistan's wicketkeeper Moin Khan

exit from the World Cup and Botham was only too eager to provide the necessary thrust. Steve Waugh and Allan Border had steered the hosts to 145 for 4 but Botham came back into the attack and grabbed four wickets in seven balls as Australia lost their last six wickets for just 26 runs. Botham had career-best ODI figures of 4 for 31 and, just to rub it in, made 54 from 77 balls – his final ODI fifty – in a century-opening stand.

New Zealand v West Indies

8 March

Twenty-first match, Auckland

THE shameless six-hitting of opener Mark Greatbatch, who earned a place only when John Wright was injured, took New Zealand almost to the ultimate glory. His most sparkling innings came at Eden Park against West Indies, on whom the hosts inflicted the third defeat of the tournament. Greatbatch launched a ferocious assault on the West Indian bowlers, deprived of their bouncers, as he mangled the quicks with devastating off-side hitting. Greatbatch hit Curtley Ambrose, Malcolm Marshall and Anderson Cummins for sixes at will. In an opening stand of 67 in 12 overs, Rod Latham scored only 14. Remembering that innings, Greatbatch said, 'Ambrose bowled quick that day. But he gave me a little bit of width, and I whacked him over point for a six. Then I struck Marshall over extra-cover for another six. That really set the tempo.'

Pakistan v South Africa

8 March

Twenty-second match, Brisbane

SOUTH AFRICA promised to bring an exciting freshness to the international scene when they finally emerged from isolation, and Jonty Rhodes stood out for his brilliance on the field. He was one of their most eye-catching players and redefined the art of fielding. Rhodes' gravity-defying, full-length dive to run out Pakistan's Inzamam-ul-Haq turned the match and was perhaps the defining moment of his career.

England v Zimbabwe

18 March

Thirty-fifth match, Albury

YOU'D be hard-pressed to locate the outback town of Albury on the map, but for one day during the 1992 World Cup it was the scene of a memorable Zimbabwean victory. On a pitch that kept low and had variable bounce, England bowled out Zimbabwe for 134, but in reply Eddo Brandes swung the ball savagely to mastermind England's collapse. First to go was Graham, who went with the first ball, LBW to a low-inswinging yorker, and two quick wickets had England sweating. Soon afterwards, he got past the defence of his best friend, Graeme Hick, whom he had warned only the last evening: 'Good luck tomorrow, but I think you'll be my bunny'. Brandes ended with 4 for 21 and, despite the lower-order resistance, England fell nine runs short in what was the biggest reversal of the World Cup, and Zimbabwe's first ODI against England.

Sri Lanka's 313 against Zimbabwe was the first and only time a team chased a total above 300.

New Zealand v Pakistan

21 March, First semi-final, Auckland

THE innings of the tournament was played by a cherubic, almost lackadaisical yet devastatingly effective Inzamam-ul-Haq. Pakistan's chances of making it to the final looked dim when they needed 123 from 15 overs at 8.2 an over, but Inzamam single-handedly changed the complexion of the match. Goaded on by the wily veteran Javed Miandad, Inzamam went berserk and slammed 60 from just 37 balls, most often shuffling across to off stump and heaving full-length deliveries over the leg side with calm audacity. The offspinner Dipak Patel, who had allowed just 28 runs from his first eight overs, haemorrhaged 22 from his last two. It was sheer carnage, and when Inzamam was run out, the target was 36 from five overs, which was passed with ease, thanks to Wasim Akram, Moin Khan and Miandad.

England v South Africa

22 March, Second semi-final, Sydney

THE second semi-final, between England and South Africa, was shaping up to be a tight, captivating game until the weather intervened near the end and a glaring mistake was shown in the rules of the tournament. Having put England in, South Africa kept them to 252 off their allocated 45 overs, with Graeme Hick scoring an excellent 83 off just 90 balls. Like England, South Africa batted as a unit and were making a good fist of their reply when the rain came. At that time, they needed 22 runs from 13 deliveries, which was a big task, but not impossible. When the rain stopped, the equation changed from 22 off 13 balls before the break to 21 off one ball! It was a farce, and the heartbroken South Africans shook their heads in disbelief, with some shedding tears.

Opposite page: Graham Gooch offers his sympathy to Brian McMillan after England's controversial win over South Africa in the semi-final at the SCG

THE FINALS England v Pakistan

25 March, Melbourne

ENGLAND had lost steam by the time they met Pakistan at the MCG, with a few leading players not at their best. Perhaps they were still a bit groggy after getting a reprieve against South Africa in the semi-final, too, for the bowlers turned in an ordinary performance in keeping Pakistan to 249. Derek Pringle started well, removing the openers, but half-centuries to Imran Khan and Javed Miandad in a stand of 139 for the third wicket in 31 overs was followed by a 52-run alliance in six overs between Inzamam-ul-Haq and Wasim Akram. That was enough to inspire Pakistan to fire on all cylinders, and their superb blend of youth and experience took care of England. The first four English batsmen were all back inside the hut with the score on 69. Neil Fairbrother and Allan Lamb attempted a middle-order recovery, but Fairbrother's dismissal by Aaqib Javed was followed by Wasim's magnificent removal of Lamb and Chris Lewis off successive deliveries. England tried to fight, but were bowled out 22 runs short, with only four balls left.

Wasim Akram emerged as one of the game's great all-rounders in the 1992 World Cup as he finished top wicket-taker with 16, and destroyed England with a Man-of-the-Match showing in the final. He went on to become one of the game's leading exponents of reverse and conventional swing, and this was best evident in the final when he snuffed out any hopes of an England win, bowling Allan Lamb and Chris Lewis with consecutive beauties.

The result of the farcical second semi-final was the adoption of the Duckworth-Lewis system.

1992

FLICK
BABAR
edges World

'The highlight of my career'

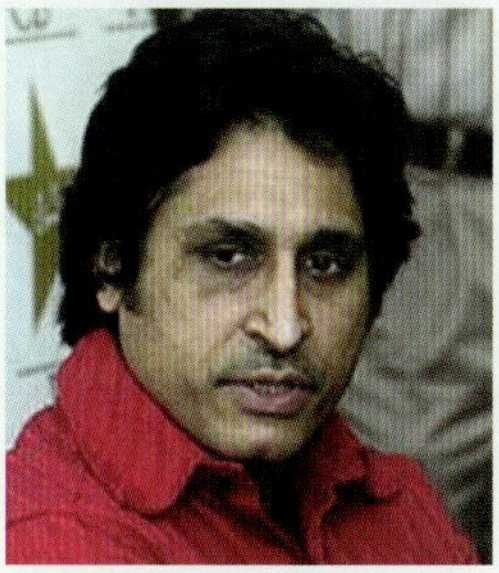

Ramiz Raja
1992 World Cup winner

DESPITE being in Australia for some time before the World Cup, and having set up a camp through which we tried to acclimatize ourselves to the conditions, Pakistan came to the 1992 World Cup with a few worries. Mushtaq Ahmed was a very narrow call for the squad; Javed Miandad was a late arrival after his back had gone out during a practice camp at home before our departure; and Waqar Younis was diagnosed with a stress fracture of the back and ruled out of the World Cup.

Then, we didn't have a great start, and I remember especially the defeat against India was very, very demoralizing. That loss had a draining effect on the team and we confined ourselves to our rooms, not least because we feared a backlash from our fans. People back home where questioning our commitment and the media was saying we had our priorities all wrong.

Meanwhile, after being beaten by West Indies, India and South Africa we were in a mental mess. But in Imran Khan we had a captain who was able to keep the team together by becoming more accessible to us. We had a meeting with some of the key players, but minus Imran, where we vowed to hit back at the critics and resurrect our image. We were determined to beat New Zealand because that was a match we could not afford to lose.

We went into that match mentally drained because we had watched the pool match between Australia and West Indies, which decided our entry into the semi-final. Knowing that we had qualified rejuvenated the team. That was a turning point for us.

Inzamam-ul-Haq was not supposed to play that match. He had not been able to sleep on the night of the game and had asked for some sleeping tablets from our coach Intikhab Alam. However, the drugs did not react well and Inzy spent the night running between the bed and the toilet. On the morning of the game, he declared himself unfit, but Imran would have nothing to do with it. In the end Imran's persistence prevailed and Inzy played the game after he was given an ultimatum that he had to bat, come what may. We all know what happened afterwards – that Inzy knock was an epic.

That is how we became finalists against England at the MCG. Before the match, we had a meeting at which Imran proudly wore the 'cornered tiger' T-shirt that he had worn in the 1987 World Cup semi-final that we lost to Australia. In that meeting, Imran spoke of the significance of the occasion and requested us all to enjoy the experience. That is when he pointed to his T-shirt and told us to play like cornered tigers.

The turning points of the final were Wasim Akram's two wickets in two balls. The decision to reintroduce Wasim into the attack was taken at the drinks break as Allan Lamb was threatening to take England to victory. Wasim first bowled a reverse outswinger to Lamb and next an incutter to Chris Lewis, and England were knocked out.

Personally, taking the last catch was a memorable moment. The stumps were being removed as I was getting underneath the catch. It was not easy, because there was the pressure of the assumption that the catch would be taken. It was difficult concentrating on the ball, but I took it and history was made. That achievement, in front of a global audience, turned each of us into an international celebrity. The love and affection we received from our nation was amazing and I will never forget that.

Opposite page: Ramiz Raja's batting in Australian conditions gave Pakistan's top order much stability

SUMMARY OF RESULTS

GROUP STAGE

England v India
at Perth – 22 February
England won by 9 runs.
England 236-9 (50 ov);
India 227 (49.2 ov)

New Zealand v Australia
at Auckland – 22 February
New Zealand won by 37 runs.
New Zealand 248-6 (50 ov);
Australia 211 (48.1 ov)

Pakistan v West Indies
at Melbourne – 23 February
West Indies won by 10 wickets.
Pakistan 220-2 (50 ov);
West Indies 221-0 (46.5 ov)

Sri Lanka v Zimbabwe
at New Plymouth – 23 February
Sri Lanka won by 3 wickets.
Zimbabwe 312-4 (50 ov);
Sri Lanka 313-7 (49.2 ov)

New Zealand v Sri Lanka
at Hamilton – 25 February
New Zealand won by 6 wickets.
Sri Lanka 206-9 (50 ov);
New Zealand 210-4 (48.2 ov)

Australia v South Africa
at Sydney – 26 February
South Africa won by 9 wickets.
Australia 170-9 (49 ov);
South Africa 171-1 (46.5 ov)

England v West Indies
at Melbourne – 27 February
England won by 6 wickets.
West Indies 157 (49.2 ov);
England 160-4 (39.5 ov)

Pakistan v Zimbabwe
at Hobart – 27 February
Pakistan won by 53 runs.
Pakistan 254-4 (50 ov);
Zimbabwe 201-7 (50 ov)

India v Sri Lanka
at Mackay – 28 February
No result.
India 1-0 (0.2 ov)

New Zealand v South Africa
at Auckland – 29 February
New Zealand won by 7 wickets.
South Africa 190-7 (50 ov);
New Zealand 191-3 (34.3 ov)

West Indies v Zimbabwe
at Brisbane – 29 February
West Indies won by 75 runs.
West Indies 264-8 (50 ov);
Zimbabwe 189-7 (50 ov)

Australia v India
at Brisbane – 1 March
Australia won by 1 run.
Australia 237-9 (50 ov);
India 234 (47 ov)

England v Pakistan
at Adelaide – 1 March
No result.
Pakistan 74 (40.2 ov);
England 24-1 (8 ov)

South Africa v Sri Lanka
at Wellington – 2 March
Sri Lanka won by 3 wickets.
South Africa 195 (50 ov);
Sri Lanka 198-7 (49.5 ov)

New Zealand v Zimbabwe
at Napier – 3 March
New Zealand won by 48 runs.
New Zealand 162-3 (20.5 ov);
Zimbabwe 105-7 (18 ov)

India v Pakistan
at Sydney – 4 March
India won by 43 runs.
India 216-7 (49 ov);
Pakistan 173 (48.1 ov)

Australia v England
at Sydney – 5 March
England won by 8 wickets.
Australia 171 (49 ov);
England 173-2 (40.5 ov)

South Africa v West Indies
at Christchurch – 5 March
South Africa won by 64 runs.
South Africa 200-8 (50 ov);
West Indies 136 (38.4 ov)

Australia v Sri Lanka
at Adelaide – 7 March
Australia won by 7 wickets.
Sri Lanka 189-9 (50 ov);
Australia 190-3 (44 ov)

India v Zimbabwe
at Hamilton – 7 March
India won by 55 runs.
India 203-7 (32 ov);
Zimbabwe 104-1 (19.1 ov)

New Zealand v West Indies
at Auckland – 8 March
New Zealand won by 5 wickets.
West Indies 203-7 (50 ov);
New Zealand 206-5 (48.3 ov).

Pakistan v South Africa
at Brisbane – 8 March
South Africa won by 20 runs.
South Africa 211-7 (50 ov);
Pakistan 173-8 (36 ov)

England v Sri Lanka
at Ballarat – 9 March
England won by 106 runs.
England 280-6 (50 ov);
Sri Lanka 174 (44 ov)

India v West Indies
at Wellington – 10 March
West Indies won by 5 wickets.
India 197 (49.4 ov);
West Indies 195-5 (40.2 ov)

South Africa v Zimbabwe
at Canberra – 10 March
South Africa won by 7 wickets.
Zimbabwe 163 (48.3 ov);
South Africa 164-3 (45.1 ov)

Australia v Pakistan
at Perth – 11 March
Pakistan won by 48 runs.
Pakistan 220-9 (50 ov);
Australia 172 (45.2 ov)

England v South Africa
at Melbourne – 12 March
England won by 3 wickets.
South Africa 236-4 (50 ov);
England 226-7 (40.5 ov)

SUMMARY OF RESULTS

GROUP STAGE

New Zealand v India
at Dunedin – 12 March
New Zealand won by 4 wickets.
India 230-6 (50 ov);
New Zealand 231-6 (47.1 ov).

India v South Africa
at Adelaide – 15 March
South Africa won by 6 wickets.
India 180-6 (30 ov);
South Africa 181-4 (29.1 ov)

Australia v West Indies
at Melbourne – 18 March
Australia won by 57 runs.
Australia 216-6 (50 ov);
West Indies 159 (42.4 ov)

Sri Lanka v West Indies
at Berri – 13 March
West Indies won by 91 runs.
West Indies 268-8 (50 ov);
Sri Lanka 177-9 (50 ov)

New Zealand v England
at Wellington – 15 March
New Zealand won by 7 wickets.
England 200-8 (50 ov);
New Zealand 201-3 (40.5 ov)

England v Zimbabwe
at Albury – 18 March
Zimbabwe won by 9 runs.
Zimbabwe 134 (46.1 ov);
England 125 (49.1 ov)

Australia v Zimbabwe
at Hobart – 14 March
Australia won by 128 runs.
Australia 265-6 (46 ov);
Zimbabwe 137 (41.4 ov)

Pakistan v Sri Lanka
at Perth – 15 March
Pakistan won by 4 wickets.
Sri Lanka 212-6 (50 ov);
Pakistan 216-6 (49.1 ov)

New Zealand v Pakistan
at Christchurch – 18 March
Pakistan won by 7 wickets.
New Zealand 166 (48.2 ov);
Pakistan 167-3 (44.4 ov)

ROUND-ROBIN STAGE TABLE

TEAM	POINTS	PLAYED	WON	LOSS	NO RESULT	RUN RATE
New Zealand	14	8	7	1	0	4.76
England	11	8	5	2	1	4.36
South Africa	10	8	5	3	0	4.36
Pakistan	9	8	4	3	1	4.33
Australia	8	8	4	4	0	4.22
West Indies	8	8	4	4	0	4.14
India	5	8	2	5	1	4.95
Sri Lanka	5	8	2	5	1	4.21
Zimbabwe	2	8	1	7	0	4.03

1ST SEMI-FINAL

New Zealand v Pakistan
at Auckland – 21 March
Pakistan won by 4 wickets.
New Zealand 262-7 (50 ov);
Pakistan 264-6 (49 ov)

2ND SEMI-FINAL

England v South Africa
at Sydney – 22 March
England won by 19 runs.
England 252-6 (45 ov);
South Africa 232-6 (43 ov)

FINAL

England v Pakistan
at Melbourne – 25 March
Pakistan won by 22 runs.
Pakistan 249-6 (50 ov);
England 227 (49.2 ov)

WILLS
LANKA

1996 India, Pakistan & Sri Lanka

Sri Lanka celebrate the wicket of Shane Warne during the 1996 final in Lahore

Sheer Lanka

THIS will forever be remembered as the World Cup where Sri Lanka shed the tag of minnows and took the global stage by storm. Along the way there were several highlights that proved the Lankans were not at the highest level to merely make up the numbers, none more exhilarating than Sanath Jayasuriya laying into new-ball attacks, and at the end of it all the endearing success of Arjuna Ranatunga's champions overcame the controversies that marred the Wills World Cup.

The tournament was embroiled in several controversies even before it began. In Sri Lanka, a bombing by the LTTE just before the event resulted in the death of 90 people. Australia and West Indies refused to travel to Colombo for their league matches, citing security concerns, and that resulted in full points for Sri Lanka as the ICC awarded the hosts both matches on grounds of forfeit.

Then, during the semi-final between India and Sri Lanka at Eden Gardens, the misbehaviour of spectators forced the match referee Clive Lloyd to award the match to Sri Lanka. In the final played in Lahore, tensions between Australia and Sri Lanka heightened after umpire Darrell Hair called Muttiah Muralitharan for a suspect bowling action.

A changed format led to the inclusion of three teams – Kenya, the Netherlands and the UAE – and an extra round, the quarter-finals. The format was not widely applauded, with critics, including players, questioning the logic of changing the successful 1992 format, a round-robin producing the top four teams. In 1996, the teams were put into two groups of six, from which eight progressed to the knock-out stage. Quite expectedly, Zimbabwe and the three minnows were eliminated. The lingering feeling was that the Wills World Cup could have been far more competitive had the previous system continued.

India and Pakistan were once again expected to go far, but neither was consistent enough. India lost to Australia and Sri Lanka in the league stage, rallied to make it to the quarter-finals, beat Pakistan in another Indo-Pak epic, but was undone by Sri Lanka in a crowd-marred semi-final. South Africa were the clear favourites after five clinical victories in the group stage, but couldn't match up against Brian Lara in the quarters; similarly, New Zealand were outdone by a classy Mark Waugh century at the same stage. England were horrible, losing all three of their games against the Test nations and struggling to beat the Netherlands.

The 15-over fielding restriction rule had made its debut in 1992, but 1996 was the year the pinch-hitters really seized their opportunity, and it was Sri Lanka, Australia and India who exploited the wide open spaces with aggressive early batting. The 1996 World Cup also saw the third umpire make his first appearance in front of the television monitor.

Nonetheless, the Lankans went on to win the World Cup by seven wickets with more than three overs to spare, thanks to a brilliant century from Aravinda de Silva. Australia had played well to reach the summit, but took their eyes off the ball when it came to play Sri Lanka in a super-charged night in Lahore. No player had dominated a World Cup final to the extent that de Silva did: he took two catches and three wickets, including Australia's top-scorers, and capped a glorious night with an unbeaten 107. Australia scored 241 for 7, a total Sri Lanka achieved in 46.2 overs. De Silva also won the Man-of-the-Match award.

Sanath Jayasuriya after scoring 82 in the quarter-final between England and Sri Lanka at Faisalabad

Opposite page: Sri Lanka captain Arjuna Ranatunga proudly displays the World Cup

Asanka Gurusinha hit the highest number of sixes (11) in six matches during this World Cup.

GROUP A: SRI LANKA, AUSTRALIA, INDIA, WEST INDIES, ZIMBABWE AND KENYA

GROUP B: SOUTH AFRICA, PAKISTAN, NEW ZEALAND, ENGLAND, UAE AND NETHERLANDS

1996

1996 Wills World Cup statistics

Formats Round robin and Knockout
Host India, Pakistan and Sri Lanka
Champions Sri Lanka (first title)
Participants 12
Matches played 37
Most runs Sachin Tendulkar (523)
Most wickets Anil Kumble (15)

Romesh Kaluwitharana only scored 73 runs in 1996.

Sachin Tendulkar lofts the ball during his 90 at the Wankhede Stadium

India v Australia

27 February

Nineteenth match, Mumbai

THE first day-night match in Mumbai was illuminated by a display of brilliant batting from two openers in prime form. Mark Waugh's 126 set up Australia's winning total of 258 and made him the first man to score successive World Cup centuries; in reply, a stroke-filled 90 from Sachin Tendulkar threatened to outdo that effort until Waugh, the bowler, took his wicket with a wide delivery. Australia had been on course for a stronger total, but Waugh's dismissal sparked a collapse of 7 for 26, four in the final over, which yielded just two runs. India's chase began poorly as Damien Fleming snared two wickets inside six overs and Glenn McGrath bowled three maidens, but Tendulkar collected three boundaries off the latter in one over and galloped from 12 to 56 in 25 balls, hitting seven fours and a six. His blazing innings was cut short by Waugh, who fired an offspinner down Tendulkar's pads for Ian Healy to effect a stumping. Fleming returned to claim 5 for 36, the 15th best figures for an Australian in ODIs. This marked Australia's first ODI win against India since the 1992 World Cup (India had won three in the meantime), Australia's first match in India since 1989, and their first win against India in India since the 1987 World Cup.

Kenya v West Indies

29 February

Twentieth match, Pune

THE roughly 5,000-strong crowd at the Nehru Stadium, despite being aware of the shambles that West Indies were in at the time, still trickled in expecting West Indies to whip Kenya, who arrived in India as 500-1 outsiders. When Kenya were dismissed for 166 after being asked to bat, it seemed West Indies were on track. Even when they lost their openers with not much on the board, few would have reacted with anxiety. But then Brian Lara gifted his wicket recklessly – nicking to the portly, bearded and bespectacled wicketkeeper, Tariq Iqbal – and Kenya kicked the door down famously. Maurice Odumbe's innocuous offspin proved to be lethal on the day and West Indies were skilled for just 93, their lowest World Cup total and their second worst in any ODI. As the Kenyans ran a high-spirited victory lap, cheered on by local spectators, West Indies realized that, level on points with Kenya and Zimbabwe, they could no longer be certain of reaching the quarter-finals. 'It's like winning the World Cup,' gushed a euphoric Odumbe. 'It's a dream come true. The West Indies are our idols, and to beat an idol is a great thing.'

England v Sri Lanka

9 March

First quarter-final, Faisalabad

SANATH JAYASURIYA took the world by storm in the 1996 World Cup, through his fearless and destructive approach at the top of the order, with his team-mate Romesh Kaluwitharana, which

Mark Waugh became the first batsman to score three hundreds in a single World Cup.

was one of the highlights of the tournament. Jayasuriya's memorable run reached its apogee during the quarter-final against England, when he bludgeoned 82 from 44 balls, including the then fastest tournament half-century, from 30 balls. His manic innings contained three sixes and 13 fours and he feasted on Ray Illingworth, whom he hit for four successive fours, and Phil DeFreitas, whose second over went for 22. When England batted, Jayasuriya had dismissed DeFreitas and Dermot Reeve and nailed a direct hit to run out Robin Smith. Sri Lanka continued their magnificent ascent, England sank; they had never been knocked out before the semi-finals in five previous World Cups.

Anil Kumble appeals for the wicket of Aamer Sohail during the quarter-final against Pakistan in Bangalore

India v Pakistan

9 March

Second quarter-final, Bangalore

THESE two arch-rivals had failed to make it to the final in 1987, and in 1996, fans on both sides of the border were served a mouth-watering knockout clash in a quarter-final in Bangalore. It was the showpiece event of the 1996 edition, and 35,000 fans were treated to a ripper. It had everything: controversy, with Pakistan captain Wasim Akram ruling himself out at the last minute; high-voltage tension; fine batting from both sides; and a little bit of spice thrown in for good measure. The first passage that few will ever forget was Ajay Jadeja's 25-ball 45. India, through Navjot Singh Sidhu's battling 93, were 168 for 2, but the run rate was hardly four and a half an over. Then Jadeja came to the fore, smashing the bowlers around the park and fuelling the lower order to ransack 51 off the last three overs. Jadeja's onslaught against Waqar Younis was electric, especially the way in which he pulled him with disdain, and the latter's final two overs cost 40 runs. Later in the evening, Saeed Anwar and stand-in-captain Aamer Sohail were threatening an early finish with some breathtaking batting, thumping 84 off the first ten overs. Even as Anwar departed, Sohail continued to tear into the attack. Having celebrated a rapid half-century with a rasping boundary past extra-cover, Sohail openly ridiculed Venkatesh Prasad as if to say, 'Go fetch that'. However, the bowler had the final laugh – and adjoining send-off – when on the very next delivery Sohail swung across the line and had his off-stump pegged back. 'Go home you f****n bastard,' was Prasad's riposte, and the Chinnaswamy Stadium erupted in a tumultuous din on realizing that it was a pivotal moment.

South Africa v West Indies

11 March

Third quarter-final, Karachi

ELEVEN days earlier, after their Pune debacle, West Indies came up against the tournament favourites, South Africa, in a

Sri Lanka's 398 for 5 against Zimbabwe in Kandy was a world record for any ODI.

Brian Lara's stroke-filled 111 ended South Africa's World Cup campaign
Opposite page: Vinod Kambli and Javagal Srinath celebrate Asanka Gurusinha's wicket during the Eden Gardens semi-final

quarter-final encounter that no-one truly believed they could win. Having been roundly criticised for his display against Kenya, Brian Lara made amends in stunning fashion. South Africa's decision to rest their spearhead Allan Donald in favour of an extra spinner, Paul Adams, proved profitable for Lara as he thrived on spin. Lara finished with 111 from 94 balls, with sixteen fours, before West Indies's own spinners, Jimmy Adams and Roger Harper, sealed the deal with 19 runs to spare.

Australia v New Zealand

11 March

Fourth quarter-final, Chennai

MARK WAUGH'S third century of the tournament – which set the record for most hundreds in a single edition of the event – was his finest. Australia needed to make the second-highest score to win a World Cup match, under below-par lights and on an outfield slowed by a damp sea mist, and Waugh replied with trademark élan. Prospering in his role as an opener, Waugh hit 110 in 112 balls to follow hundreds in the group games against Kenya and India. It was one of the coolest, breeziest hundreds ever; Waugh's easy-on-the-eye stroke play complimented his steely grit in just about two-and-a-half hours of nimble-footed driving and flicking, Waugh showcased his easy elegance. The target of 287 was a daunting one, but Waugh batted beautifully to make a complete mockery of it.

UAE captain Sultan Zarawani was the only member of the team to be born in the UAE.

There were 16 centuries scored in the 1996 World Cup.

THE SEMI-FINALS

Sri Lanka v India

13 March, First semi-final, Calcutta

SRI LANKA had beaten India easily in their league match, and when the two teams squared off in front of a Kolkata crowd of 110,000 in the first semi-final, tensions were high. Mindful of the ease with which Sri Lanka had chased 272 in Delhi, Mohammad Azharuddin put the opposition in and when both openers were dismissed in four deliveries the Indians were cock-a-hoop. Then Aravinda de Silva played an amazing innings. With a seeming disregard for the horror start Sri Lanka had been inflicted, de Silva shut out the roars of a partisan Eden Gardens din and raced to his fifty off just 32 balls. It was a graceful innings punctuated by 11 boundaries, none with any ferocity. De Silva's driving was especially pleasing, with the ball repeatedly caressed between cover and extra-cover as the Indians were left for retrieval purposes only. All the while the run rate hovered near seven, even as Asanka Gurusinga laboured 29 minutes and 16 balls for a single run. De Silva was finally bowled for 66 off 47 balls in the 15th over, inside-edging Anil Kumble onto his stumps. From 85 for 3, Sri Lanka rallied to 251 for 8 on a rapidly waning wicket. De Silva later picked up a wicket as India's World Cup dreams came crashing down after passionate fans failed to digest an infamous collapse and expressed themselves by throwing water bottles and other projectiles, as well as setting fire to the seating.

Australia v West Indies

14 March, Second semi-final, Mohali

IT was a stunning comeback for Australia: from the depths of 15 for 4, Stuart Law and Michael Bevan got down and dirty, and resuscitated the innings to 207 for 8. It all looked like going pear-shaped for the Aussies when West Indies cruised to 165 for 2 in the 42nd over, needing 63 from the last nine, but then that crafty magician Shane Warne got into the act, plucking three wickets from nowhere in three mesmerizing overs. West Indies folded spectacularly, losing eight wickets in the final 50 minutes. Brian Lara fell for 45, Roger Harper and Ottis Gibson failed to fire, Jimmy Adams and Keith Arthurton appeared overawed. Richie Richardson hung on with the last man Courtney Walsh until the last over, bowled by Damien Fleming, with West Indies needing 6 runs. It wasn't to be, and West Indies had lost 8 for 37 in 50 balls. After the match, Mark Taylor candidly stated that West Indies had won 95 per cent of the match.

Opposite page: Sri Lankan players celebrate a wicket during the final

THE FINALS Australia v Sri Lanka

17 March, Lahore

THIS is Sri Lankan cricket's most famous day. Having played aggressive, attractive cricket, the team from the Emerald Isle found themselves up against Australia at a packed Gaddafi Stadium. India and Pakistan had failed to reach the summit and, thus, Sri Lanka were now Asia's only hope. Winning the toss to a loud cheer, Arjuna Ranatunga changed his tactics of batting first to allow Sanath Jayasuriya first use of the deck and opted to field. When Mark Taylor led a strong start to 137 for 1, it appeared Ranatunga had grossly erred. But then his spinner rallied, led by Aravinda de Silva's canny offbreaks that yielded Taylor's wicket, out sweeping, and a spell of 19 for 2 from five overs. Aggressive fielding and tight bowling stifled Australia's efforts, limiting the favourites to 241, which seemed plenty when Sri Lanka's openers were gone with just 23 runs on the board. But this was de Silva's day; after three wickets, he batted his way to an unbeaten century with able support from Asanka Gurusinha and Ranatunga, who steered the winning runs to seal a sensational win that was cheered by 23,826 spectators.

Sachin Tendulkar top-scored 523 runs in seven matches at an average of 87.17.

Anil Kumble was the highest wicket-taker with 15 at 18.74. Waqar Younis took 13 wickets at 19.46.

SRI LANK
USTRALIA

‘Management and leadership, the key’

Ranjit Fernando
Former Sri Lankan cricketer turned commentator

Generally Sri Lankans are laid back, but give them a challenge or an issue to rally round, and they are all unified and prepared to fully back the cause. The calling of Muttiah Muralitharan by umpire Daryl Hair in Australia a few months before the 1996 World Cup was the ideal tonic and it not only brought the team together, but also saw the entire country united, waiting for the World Cup, to get their own back.

Sri Lanka beat India convincingly in the preliminary round, and that was just the right beginning. With Australia and West Indies not visiting Sri Lanka, and Kenya getting a severe drubbing in Kandy, the stage was well set, and the optimism started soaring, right from the outset.

The half allrounders and the ‘bits and pieces’ players were crucial for Sri Lanka, and it gave great balance to the team, in the absence of any worthwhile quick bowlers, apart from Chaminda Vaas. On subcontinent tracks Sanath Jayasuriya and Aravinda de Silva were very handy bowlers, and were in a sense underrated by the opposition. This stood as a distinct advantage, together with Kumar Dharmasena who was extremely difficult to score runs off in the subcontinent. When you have two world-class batsmen like Jayasuriya and de Silva able to bowl five or six overs each, in a World Cup, and also pick up wickets, what more could you ask for?

Further, Dav Whatmore’s contribution to the team cannot be emphasized enough. When Dav took over as the first full-time permanent coach, the Sri Lankan team was already on the move and getting close to the pinnacle. The team was well balanced, batted very deep, with a number of world-class players, and the half allrounders also gave it many bowling options. The fielding was world-class with Roshan Mahanama, Hashan Tillekeratne, Asanka Gurusinghe, Jayasuriya, Murali and de Silva all outstanding. Arjuna Ranatunga was well entrenched in the job as captain, and was well in control with his deputy de Silva. Sri Lanka had already won their first series abroad against New Zealand.

Opposite page: Aravinda de Silva celebrates after reaching his century during the final in Lahore

A temperamentally suited, full-time, permanent coach who understood Sri Lankan culture, with a long-term plan for a consistency and strategy was the need of the hour, and Dav came in at the right time. He was always available to the players and brought in a degree of professionalism and continuity which was not there before. Planning and organisation received greater attention, and this was his biggest contribution. The fitness culture and regimes took an entirely new approach, with Whatmore bringing in physiotherapist/trainer Alex Kontouri.

Then, Ranatunga’s role in Sri Lanka’s success deserves special mention. There is no doubt that he changed the culture, in the way the Sri Lankans approached their cricket. Under him, our cricketers quickly changed from being ‘nice boys” to a team of fierce competitors, who took on the oppositions’ antics, in their characteristic style. Arjuna himself showed the way, and consequently was not always very popular with them. His philosophy was that someone had to do the job, and as a leader it was his responsibility. As all good leaders, he stood by his men, at times putting his neck on the line. He wanted to make winning to be a habit.

Jayasuriya’s entertainment and de Silva’s masterful batting (four Man-of-the-match awards) were the highlight of the 1996 World Cup. Of course, the Ranatunga-de Silva partnership in the final, to take Sri Lanka to victory, was something that cannot be forgotten.

SUMMARY OF RESULTS

GROUP STAGE

Group B: England v New Zealand
at Ahmedabad – 14 February
New Zealand won by 11 runs.
New Zealand 239-6 (50 ov);
England 228-9 (50 ov)

Group A: West Indies v Zimbabwe
at Hyderabad – 16 February
West Indies won by 6 wickets.
Zimbabwe 151-9 (50 ov);
West Indies 155-4 (29.3 ov)

Group B: South Africa v UAE
at Rawalpindi – 16 February
South Africa won by 169 runs.
South Africa 321-2 (50 ov);
UAE 152-8 (50 ov)

Group A: Sri Lanka v Australia
at Colombo – 17 February
Sri Lanka won by a walkover.

Group B: Netherlands v New Zealand
at Vadodara – 17 February
New Zealand won by 119 runs.
New Zealand 307-8 (50 ov);
Netherlands 188-7 (50 ov)

Group A: India v Kenya
at Cuttack – 18 February
India won by 7 wickets.
Kenya 199-6 (50 ov);
India 203-3 (41.5 ov)

Group B: England v UAE
at Peshawar – 18 February
England won by 8 wickets.
UAE 136 (48.3 ov);
England 140-2 (35 ov)

Group B: New Zealand v South Africa
at Faisalabad – 20 February
South Africa won by 5 wickets.
New Zealand 177-9 (50 ov);
South Africa 178-5 (37.3 ov)

Group A: India v West Indies
at Gwalior – 21 February
India won by 5 wickets.
West Indies 173 (50 ov);
India 174-5 (39.4 ov)

Group A: Sri Lanka v Zimbabwe
at Colombo – 21 February
Sri Lanka won by 6 wickets.
Zimbabwe 228-6 (50 ov);
Sri Lanka 229-4 (37 ov).

Group B: England v Netherlands
at Peshawar – 22 February
England won by 49 runs.
England 279-4 (50 ov);
Netherlands 230-6 (50 ov)

Group A: Australia v Kenya
at Visakhapatnam – 23 February
Australia won by 97 runs.
Australia 304-7 (50 ov);
Kenya 207-7 (50 ov)

Group B: Pakistan v United Arab Emirates at
Gujranwala – 24 February
Pakistan won by 9 wickets.
UAE 109-9 (33 ov);
Pakistan 112-1 (18 ov)

Group A: Sri Lanka v West Indies
at Colombo – 25 February
Sri Lanka won by a walkover.

Group B: England v South Africa
at Rawalpindi – 25 February
South Africa won by 78 runs.
South Africa 230 (50 ov);
England 152 (44.3 ov)

Group A (replayed): Kenya v Zimbabwe
at Patna – 26 February
No result.
Zimbabwe 45-3 (15.5 ov)

Group B: Pakistan v Netherlands
at Lahore – 26 February
Pakistan won by 8 wickets.
Netherlands 145-7 (50 ov);
Pakistan 151-2 (30.4 ov)

Group A: India v Australia
at Mumbai – 27 February
Australia won by 16 runs.
Australia 258 (50 ov);
India 242 (48 ov)

Group A: Kenya v Zimbabwe
at Patna – 27 February
Zimbabwe won by 5 wickets.
Kenya 134 (49.4 ov);
Zimbabwe 137-5 (42.2 ov)

Group B: New Zealand v UAE
at Faisalabad – 27 February
New Zealand won by 109 runs.
New Zealand 276-8 (47 ov);
UAE 167-9 (47 ov)

Group A: Kenya v West Indies
at Poona – 29 February
Kenya won by 73 runs.
Kenya 166 (49.3 ov);
West Indies 93 (35.2 ov)

Group B: Pakistan v South Africa
at Karachi – 29 February
South Africa won by 5 wickets.
Pakistan 242-6 (50 ov);
South Africa 243-5 (44.2 ov)

Group A: Australia v Zimbabwe
at Nagpur – 1 March
Australia won by 8 wickets.
Zimbabwe 154 (45.3 ov);
Australia 158-2 (36 ov)

Group B: Netherlands v UAE
at Lahore – 1 March
UAE won by 7 wickets.
Netherlands 216-9 (50 ov);
UAE 220-3 (44.2 ov)

SUMMARY OF RESULTS

GROUP STAGE

Group A: India v Sri Lanka
at Delhi – 2 March
Sri Lanka won by 6 wickets.
India 271-3 (50 ov);
Sri Lanka 272-4 (48.4 ov)

Group B: Pakistan v England
at Karachi – 3 March
Pakistan won by 7 wickets.
England 249-9 (50 ov);
Pakistan 250-3 (47.4 ov)

Group A: Australia v West Indies
at Jaipur – 4 March
West Indies won by 4 wickets.
Australia 229-6 (50 ov);
West Indies 232-6 (48.5 ov)

Group B: Netherlands v South Africa
at Rawalpindi – 5 March
South Africa won by 160 runs.
South Africa 328-3 (50 ov);
Netherlands 168-8 (50 ov)

Group A: India v Zimbabwe
at Kanpur – 6 March
India won by 40 runs.
India 247-5 (50 ov);
Zimbabwe 207 (49.4 ov)

Group A: Sri Lanka v Kenya
at Kandy – 6 March
Sri Lanka won by 144 runs.
Sri Lanka 398-5 (50 ov);
Kenya 254-7 (50 ov)

Group B: Pakistan v New Zealand
at Lahore – 6 March
Pakistan won by 46 runs.
Pakistan 281-5 (50 ov);
New Zealand 235 (47.3 ov)

SUMMARY OF RESULTS

GROUP A

TEAM	POINTS	PLAYED	WON	LOSS	NO RESULT	RUN RATE
Sri Lanka	10	5	5	0	0	1.60
Australia	6	5	3	2	0	0.90
India	6	5	3	2	0	0.45
West Indies	4	5	2	3	0	-0.13
Zimbabwe	2	5	1	4	0	-0.93
Kenya	2	5	1	4	0	-1.00

GROUP B

TEAM	POINTS	PLAYED	WON	LOSS	NO RESULT	RUN RATE
South Africa	10	5	5	0	0	2.04
Pakistan	8	5	4	1	0	0.96
New Zealand	6	5	3	2	0	0.55
England	4	5	2	3	0	0.08
UAE	2	5	1	4	0	-1.83
Netherlands	0	5	0	5	0	-1.92

Shane Warne fails to make his crease and is run out during the final

1ST QUARTER-FINAL
England v Sri Lanka at Faisalabad
– 9 March
Sri Lanka won by 5 wickets.
England 235-8 (50 ov);
Sri Lanka 236-5 (40.4 ov)

2ND QUARTER-FINAL
India v Pakistan at Bangalore
– 9 March
India won by 39 runs.
India 287-8 (50 ov);

1ST SEMI-FINAL
India v Sri Lanka at Calcutta
– 13 March
Sri Lanka won (match conceded).
Sri Lanka 251-8 (50 ov);
India 120-8 (34.1 ov)

2ND SEMI-FINAL
Australia v West Indies at Mohali
– 14 March
Australia won by 5 runs.
Australia 207-8 (50 ov);

1999 England, Scotland, Ireland & Netherlands

Steve Waugh's Australia are jubilant after clinching the World Cup at Lord's

We Warned You

THE idea behind getting back the World Cup to England was to revive interest in the 50-over game in the country. However, the host country made no impact at all. Just 16 days into the World Cup, with 21 to go, England were ousted and hardly anyone in the country even knew. That the remaining matches found spectators, and a $51 million profit was declared, is testament to the success of the tournament. Adding the maximum flavour were Indian, Pakistani and Sri Lankan expats, whose vibrancy was unrivalled in the history of World Cups held in England. Though there was some criticism of the loyalty of these British Asians, most infamously by the Tory cabinet minister Norman Tebbitt, it became evident that it was this community that loved their cricket the most. Thus the 1999 World Cup was deemed a success despite a new format that initially appeared attractive, but whose flaws became evident as the tournament progressed.

Having failed at the summit four years ago, Australia at one stage of the summer looked set to crash out of the World Cup. Defeats to New Zealand and Pakistan meant Steve Waugh's team had to beat West Indies to progress to the Super Six, a complex round that replaced the quarter-finals, and they did so stirringly to gain some momentum. They had a bit of luck, for a tied semi-final granted them access to the final on the basis of a superior net run rate than South Africa's.

The idea behind doing away with the quarter-finals – credited to Terry Blake, the England and Wales Cricket Board's marketing head – was to make the tournament format smoother than that in 1996. Ironically, more matches were played this time around and compared to a 33-day tournament in 1996, the summer of 1999 lasted 37 days, with matches also played in Holland and Scotland. Blake's idea divided 12 teams into two groups of six, with the top three from each progressing to the Super Six. This wasn't an entirely appreciated move, because teams could only carry forward points earned against the two other qualifying teams from that group.

Geoff Allott, the tournament's highest wicket taker, in action

Attracting further criticism was the rule applied to the epic tie-breaker in the Edgbaston semi-final, which Australia won owing to a superior net run rate of +0.358, compared with South Africa's +0.174.

The associate teams gained little from this tournament, even though Bangladesh stunned Pakistan in an inconsequential match at Northampton. West Indies were outright failures, and there were flashes of brilliance from New Zealand, Zimbabwe and South Africa along the way as heavyweight teams like India and Sri Lanka disappointed. New Zealand, without being flashy, worked their way into the semis on the basis of some sharp cricket, especially from their seamers in favourable conditions: Geoff Allott's 20 wickets were a tournament highlight and broke the previous record of 18. South Africa began strongly, but petered out before making it to the semis, in which they were ousted in that most thrilling of ties. Zimbabwe were the biggest surprise of the summer, beating India and South Africa, and so nearly making it to the final four. Leading their cause was the all-rounder Neil Johnson, one of the successes of the tournament.

Pakistan landed up in the final despite losing three games in a row, one in the league and two in the Super Six stage. When it mattered, however, they trampled over Zimbabwe and New Zealand to qualify for the final. But the final was a one-sided affair, with Australia running away to victory. Pakistan could only muster 132 as Warne mesmerized again with four wickets, dismissing Ijaz Ahmed, Moin Khan, Shahid Afridi and Wasim Akram from nine overs. This performance earned him the Man-of-the-Match award. The first World Cup final, at Lord's 24 years earlier almost to the day, had lasted nearly ten hours. This one lasted a little over five. The best Test team in the world was crowned ODI champion, the first time in 16 years that a side had earned that title.

Mark Ealham became the first bowler to take a wicket off his very first ball in the World Cup.

Shoaib Akhtar was at his best during the semi-final against New Zealand at Old Trafford

GROUP A: SOUTH AFRICA, INDIA, ZIMBABWE, SRI LANKA, ENGLAND, KENYA

GROUP B: PAKISTAN, NEW ZEALAND, AUSTRALIA, WEST INDIES, BANGLADESH, SCOTLAND

1999 ICC World Cup statistics

Formats Round robin and Knockout
Host England, Scotland, Ireland and Netherlands
Champions Australia (second title)
Participants 12
Matches played 42
Most runs Rahul Dravid (421)
Most wickets Geoff Allott (20), Shane Warne (20)

For the first time in World Cup history, the opening match did not have an individual hundred.

Sourav Ganguly and Rahul Dravid added a record partnership against Sri Lanka at Taunton

Australia v New Zealand
20 May
Tenth match, Cardiff

THE first upset of the tournament came between Trans-Tasman rivals at Sophia Gardens, hosting its first ODI. Under overcast conditions and on a drowsy pitch, Geoff Allott and Gavin Larsen proved hard to get away, and Australia stumbled to 213 for 8. When New Zealand came out to chase, the skies had parted and the sun beat down on the field; thus, batting was much easier, and even though Australia tried to make a fist of it, New Zealand recovered from 49 for 4. Starring were Chris Cairns and Roger Twose, who together forged a match-winning stand of 148 that allowed victory with 28 balls remaining. Twose was efficient in hitting an unbeaten 80, while Cairns lived up to his reputation with a pugnacious innings, highlighted by a six off Shane Warne that sailed out of the ground and into the river Taff.

India v Kenya
23 May
Fifteenth match, Bristol

A facile win was set up in stirring manner by Sachin Tendulkar and Rahul Dravid, thereby keeping India in the mix for the Super Six. It was eye-moistening stuff: Tendulkar had only just returned a day before from India having cremated his father. His appearance at 92 for 2 drew a raucous applause, and his batting left everyone captivated. Tendulkar batted 'in the zone', reaching his 50 off 54 balls and a century off 84. The last ball of the Indian innings was flicked over midwicket for six as Tendulkar ended on 140 from 101 balls, his 22nd century and first as a non-opener. Giving him excellent support in a record 237-run stand in 29 overs was Dravid, with an elegant century that almost when unnoticed. It was Tendulkar's day completely. When he looked skyward upon reaching three figures and later dedicated the knock to his father's memory, it was difficult not to feel a lump in the throat.

Sri Lanka v India
26 May
Twenty-first match, Taunton

SRI LANKA in 1999 were a far cry from the Sri Lanka of 1996. Most glaringly, they seemed incapable of adapting to overcast conditions

Venkatesh Prasad's 5 for 27 v Pakistan broke the previous best figures by an Indian in a World Cup.

and skiddy surfaces, where going over the top inside the first 15 overs wasn't as easy as in Asia. And it was at Taunton that they most famously fell apart, oddly enough on the most batting-friendly track of the tournament. Sri Lanka's bowlers were erratic and Sourav Ganguly and Rahul Dravid tore them apart en route to a world record partnership of 318 in 45 overs, the best alliance in ODI history. Ganguly's 183 in 156 balls, whose last 83 runs came in just 39 balls, was the second best for a World Cup and India's total of 373 for 6, the second best in ODIs. Dravid was in sublime form as he reached his second successive century at nearly a run a ball. It was sublime batting, and Sri Lanka were never in with a chance once their openers were out inside five overs.

Shane Warne was mesmerizing during the summer of 1999

South Africa v Zimbabwe
29 May
Twenty-sixth match, Chelmsford

ZIMBABWE were a team to reckon with by 1999, and their biggest scalp of the tournament was South Africa. Starring with the ball on this historic day was Neil Johnson, who had represented South Africa before returning to his motherland, with a fine all-round performance. Opening the innings after Zimbabwe had opted to bat, Johnson struck a sparky 76 full of hard-hit drives and was especially severe on Jacques Kallis with the new ball. Zimbabwe struggled thereafter and posted 234, a total which Johnson made to appear way too much for a strong South African outfit. His first delivery reared up at Gary Kirsten and Andy Whittall took a good catch at gully, the first of three he would pouch. Kallis fell fourth ball and Cronje was yorked; South Africa were in disarray at 40 for 6. Zimbabwe went on to hand South Africa their first defeat of the tournament and moved to the second stage of a World Cup for the first time.

Australia v West Indies
30 May
Twenty-eighth match, Old Trafford

LIKE Australia, Glenn McGrath had spluttered during the initial stages of the World Cup. Having lost to New Zealand and Pakistan, the Aussies reached Old Trafford knowing they had to beat West Indies to gain entry into the Super Six Stage.

Shane Warne's 21 runs to Robin Singh and Ajay Jadeja were the most by an Australian in an over.

Steve Waugh's magnificent century against South Africa kept Australia alive
Opposite page: Pakistan's Saqlain Mushtaq claimed a hat-trick against Zimbabwe at The Oval

It was here that McGrath, having written in a newspaper column that he would negate Brian Lara's threat and take five wickets, chose to step up and rally the troops to a morale-boosting victory. He really was at his best on a juicy track: from the first ball, McGrath had West Indies hopping and they had no answer to his metronomic bowling, folding for just 110. Lara came to the middle needing to avert a hat-trick (Sherwin Campbell and Jimmy Adams had perished) and though he did so, McGrath would have his number for 9 with a superb delivery that shaped away and clipped the top of the off stump. Three wickets had fallen to McGrath in 14 deliveries, and he returned to fulfil his prophecy of a five – for later in the innings.

Pakistan v Zimbabwe

11 June

Seventh Super Six match, The Oval, London

PAKISTAN had lost three successive matches, but had judged their defeats so well that they still qualified at the top of the Super Six. And it was at The Oval that they eased into the semi-finals with a comprehensive team performance. Zimbabwe were playing their third match in six days and it showed: Saeed Anwar reeled off a fluent century and after Heath Streak attempted to pull Pakistan back with his hundredth ODI wicket, the first Zimbabwean to do so, the wheels came off as Shahid Afridi smoked a breezy 37 to get the score to 271. From the time Shoaib Akhtar shattered Grant Flower's stumps, the writing was on the wall. Three wickets to Abdur Razzaq were followed by Saqlain Mushtaq ending the innings with the second World Cup hat-trick. This win set the tone for Pakistan's ascendancy into the final.

Australia v South Africa

13 June

Ninth Super Six match, Headingley

WITH his captaincy on the line, Steve Waugh chose Headingley for arguably the greatest innings seen in a World Cup. Australia had snuck into the Super Sixes on the back of defeats to Pakistan and New Zealand; and wins over India and Zimbabwe had resurrected them mathematically, but they had to beat South Africa to reach the semi-finals. On the eve of this match, Shane Warne had warned his team-mates not to walk if they were to offer a catch to Herschelle Gibbs. 'He has a tendency to flick the ball away before accepting it properly,' said Warne, only to be greeted with mocking laughs. Come game day, and it was Gibbs who set up a chase of 272 with an excellent century. South Africa then had Australia at 48 for 3, when Waugh strode to the middle. Waugh reached his fifty from 47 balls, but on 56 flicked Lance Klusener to midwicket. Gibbs easily took the catch, but in his excitement to celebrate, he dropped the ball as he threw it up in the air. Waugh's reaction was: 'I hope you realise that you've just lost the game for your team'. Waugh finished with an unbeaten 120 as victory was clinched with two balls to spare.

Chris Harris' 3.1-0-7-4 against Scotland were the best in the World Cup.

The West Indies-Scotland match was the shortest ever in ODI and World Cup history.

THE SEMI-FINALS

New Zealand v Pakistan

16 June, First semi-final, Old Trafford

OLD TRAFFORD was witness to a lop-sided affair, thanks mainly to an all-out, devil-may-care, floppy-haired speedster called Shoaib Akhtar. Having just shot to prominence with a fiery spell in a pre-World Cup series in India, Shoaib chose a venue that was more Karachi than Manchester – it was the hottest day of the tournament, the surface was hard and dry, and a 20,000-strong sea of green and white blared instruments – to stamp his claim as the fastest and most exciting bowler in the game. Consistently topping 90 mph, Shoaib bowled three spells, 4-3-3, and cleaned up a batsman in each. With his 15th ball, Nathan Astle, reduced to fishing and hopping for the first of his 17 deliveries, had his leg stump flattened by an express delivery that burst through his airborne defence. When Shoaib returned to a tumultuous roar, he served up the ball of the match, if not the entire tournament. It was a yorker, 92 mph and moving, and Stephen Fleming jammed his bat down on it about an hour to late. Leg stump went packing, the crowd erupted, the bowler celebrated. One final spell remained, and sure enough, Shoaib came back on in the 46th over, around the stumps, and took out a clueless Chris Harris's leg stump with a devilishly disguised slower one. He showed pace does matter in one-day cricket, Wasim Akram proudly declared.

Australia v South Africa

17 June, Second semi-final, Edgbaston

IT'S the stuff of folklore; the bizarre last over, with the two boundaries hammered by Lance Klusener, the inexplicable mix-up with Allan Donald, the scores tied. But anyone who was at Birmingham that day will say that it belonged to Shane Warne. Five months after a return from shoulder injury, Warne bowled a spell eerily reminiscent of the semi-finals of the previous World Cup, when victory had threatened to slip out of Australia's reach. South Africa, chasing 213, were 43 for 0 with Herschelle Gibbs and Gary Kirsten looking good when Warne was tossed the ball. Ambling in, he unleashed a beauty. The ball looped up, drifted away, landed in the rough outside leg stump, and fizzed past a dumbfounded Gibbs to clip off. Gibbs could only stand in disbelief, refusing to acknowledge that he had been bowled. Five deliveries later, Warne floated another one up in the footmarks outside leg, Kirsten went down to sweep, missed, and the ball hit off again. Hansie Cronje lasted just two deliveries, as an attempted flick to the onside went to first slip and Warne had three wickets in eight balls. Called back for his final spell, Warne added Jacques Kallis to his kitty and a spell of 4 for 29 had been completed.

Opposite page: Glenn McGrath gave Australia an early breakthrough at Lord's with the wicket of Pakistan opener Wajahatullah Wasti

THE FINALS Australia v Pakistan 20 June, Lord's, London

AUSTRALIA had reached the finals needing to win their last seven matches. They had almost seen Gibbs end their tournament. They had done so much in the days leading up to the final that their determination and professionalism was profound. Pakistan, conversely, appeared overwhelmed by pressure of adversity on the big stage and never climbed out of the hole they dug for themselves. Winning the toss was about all that went Pakistan's way. On a damp wicket, Saeed Anwar briefly fluttered but once, Mark Waugh took a blinder to get rid of an itchy Wajahatullah Wasti; the wobble was on. A bat grip change for Anwar resulted in a manic slash the very next ball, and Pakistan were 21 for 2. Razzaq's promotion to No. 3 resulted in a laborious 17 from 51 balls; no Pakistani batsman was able to cope with a discipline attack on a sluggish pitch; and Australia found themselves needing to chase 133 with plenty of time in hand. Gilchrist stormed out eager to finish the match and head home. early; he rattled away 54 off 46 balls as Australia cruised to 75 for 1 in the 11th over. The total was chased in 21 overs with eight wickets remaining.

The 51 extras conceded by India to Zimbabwe at Leicester was a new record in World Cup history.

Lance Klusener smashed 281 runs at 140.5 in the tournament and was only dismissed twice.

'Underdogs, but not underachievers'

Geoff Allott

1999 World Cup semi-finalist and highest wicket-taker of the tournament

The summer of 1999 was a special one for me, as I felt that I could directly contribute to the success of the team. I had pretty ordinary skills, so I guess it reinforced in me that desire and passion can play a big part in success. The conditions suited me early on, but many people didn't realize that it was only in the preceding months that I had learnt to bowl a consistent inswinger. The grip with which I used to hold the ball was a bit unconventional, but it helped with my wrist alignment and, therefore, the swing of the ball. As part of our buildup to the tournament, we had managed to get a few Duke balls in New Zealand for training purposes, which had swing; so I was just hopeful that it continued when we got to England – needless to say I was relieved when it did!

To get the World Cup record with a player of Shane Warne's calibre was amazing. While it was disappointing from my perspective that I could only pick up one wicket in my last two games, it was really exciting watching live at Lord's as Shane and Glenn McGrath in the final closed in on twenty wickets. I was with John Graham (our manager) at the time and he wanted me to remain the highest wicket-taker on my own, but I must admit, I wasn't too disappointed to have Shane's name beside mine!

The key for me that summer was my personal confidence and the support from the bowlers at the other end, particularly Dion Nash during the World Cup – he was great. We were fortunate enough to go on from that tour and win a Test match for the first time at Lord's and win a Test series in England for only the second time in our history. It was an outstanding time to be involved in New Zealand cricket.

Opposite page: Geoff Allott's 20 wickets were instrumental in a solid New Zealand team making the semi-finals

The conditions early on definitely favoured me, but it was interesting to note how quickly the wickets started drying out. The game against Australia was definitely the highlight for me. Firstly, it was an important result for us because points from teams that you beat in the first round carried through to the Super Six round and, secondly, to get out Adam Gilchrist, Mark Waugh, Michael Bevan and Warne was special.

The game against Scotland was interesting in that we had to bowl them out cheaply and then score the runs quickly to qualify, so to be Man of the Match in that game was nice (the only time I achieved this for New Zealand). I was confident going into the game, but it relied on the entire team to perform to ensure we qualified.

Our run ended in Manchester and it was very, very disappointing. I was ineffective and it was a huge disappointment. Pakistan shut us completely with both ball and bat, and they thoroughly deserved their victory. I will never forget the crowd – amazing – 85 per cent of the Pakistani contingent went absolutely berserk as they closed in on victory. In all honesty, there was no satisfaction.

Stephen Fleming proved over the years just how good a captain he was. Unlike many others in the world, he had the task of managing a side that, in world terms, was inconsistent. Thus, despite this being a successful period for New Zealand cricket (i.e. semi-finalists at the 1999 World Cup, a Test series win in England that year, and winning the ICC Champions Trophy in 2000 in Kenya), he had plenty on his plate to deal with outside of cricket and that couldn't have made it easy.

We believed we could win the World Cup if we had put a complete performance together, so it was disappointing. I believe our team was talented enough, despite there being some incredible players at the tournament. But we just didn't quite get it right.

SUMMARY OF RESULTS

GROUP STAGE

Group A: England v Sri Lanka
at Lord's – 14 May
England won by 8 wickets.
Sri Lanka 204 (48.4 ov);
England 207-2 (46.5 ov)

Group A: India v South Africa
at Hove – 15 May
South Africa won by 4 wickets.
India 253-5 (50 ov);
South Africa 254-6 (47.2 ov)

Group A: Kenya v Zimbabwe
at Taunton – 15 May
Zimbabwe won by 5 wickets.
Kenya 229-7 (50 ov);
Zimbabwe 231-5 (41 ov)

Group B: Australia v Scotland
at Worcester – 16 May
Australia won by 6 wickets.
Scotland 181-7 (50 ov);
Australia 182-4 (44.5 ov)

Group B: Pakistan v West Indies
at Bristol – 16 May
Pakistan won by 27 runs.
Pakistan 229-8 (50 ov);
West Indies 202 (48.5 ov)

Group B: Bangladesh v New Zealand
at Chelmsford – 17 May
New Zealand won by 6 wickets.
Bangladesh 116 (37.4 ov);
New Zealand 117-4 (33 ov)

Group A: England v Kenya
at Canterbury – 18 May
England won by 9 wickets.
Kenya 203 (49.4 ov);
England 204-1 (39 ov)

Group A: India v Zimbabwe
at Leicester – 19 May
Zimbabwe won by 3 runs.
Zimbabwe 252-9 (50 ov);
India 249 (45 ov)

Group A: South Africa v Sri Lanka
at Northampton – 19 May
South Africa won by 89 runs.
South Africa 199-9 (50 ov);
Sri Lanka 110 (35.2 ov)

Group B: Australia v New Zealand
at Cardiff – 20 May
New Zealand won by 5 wickets.
Australia 213-8 (50 ov);
New Zealand 214-5 (45.2 ov)

Group B: Pakistan v Scotland
at Chester-le-Street – 20 May
Pakistan won by 94 runs.
Pakistan 261-6 (50 ov);
Scotland 167 (38.5 ov)

Group B: Bangladesh v West Indies
at Dublin – 21 May
West Indies won by 7 wickets.
Bangladesh 182 (49.2 ov);
West Indies 183-3 (46.3 ov)

Group A: England v South Africa
at The Oval – 22 May
South Africa won by 122 runs.
South Africa 225-7 (50 ov);
England 103 (41 ov)

Group A: Sri Lanka v Zimbabwe
at Worcester – 22 May
Sri Lanka won by 4 wickets.
Zimbabwe 197-9 (50 ov);
Sri Lanka 198-6 (46 ov)

Group A: India v Kenya
at Bristol – 23 May
India won by 94 runs.
India 329-2 (50 ov);
Kenya 235-7 (50 ov)

Group B: Australia v Pakistan
at Leeds – 23 May
Pakistan won by 10 runs.
Pakistan 275-8 (50 ov);
Australia 265 (49.5 ov)

Group B: New Zealand v West Indies
at Southampton – 24 May
West Indies won by 7 wickets.
New Zealand 156 (48.1 ov);
West Indies 158-3 (44.2 ov)

Group B: Scotland v Bangladesh
at Edinburgh – 24 May
Bangladesh won by 22 runs.
Bangladesh 185-9 (50 ov);
Scotland 163 (46.2 ov)

Group A: England v Zimbabwe
at Nottingham – 25 May
England won by 7 wickets.
Zimbabwe 167-8 (50 ov);
England 168-3 (38.3 ov)

Group A: India v Sri Lanka
at Taunton – 26 May
India won by 157 runs.
India 373-6 (50 ov);
Sri Lanka 216 (42.3 ov)

Group A: Kenya v South Africa
at Amstelveen – 26 May
South Africa won by 7 wickets.
Kenya 152 (44.3 ov);
South Africa 153-3 (41 ov)

Group B: Australia v Bangladesh
at Chester-le-Street – 27 May
Australia won by 7 wickets.
Bangladesh 178-7 (50 ov);
Australia 181-3 (19.5 ov)

Group B: Scotland v West Indies
at Leicester – 27 May
West Indies won by 8 wickets.
Scotland 68 (31.3 ov);
West Indies 70-2 (10.1 ov)

Group B: New Zealand v Pakistan
at Derby – 28 May
Pakistan won by 62 runs.
Pakistan 269-8 (50 ov);
New Zealand 207-8 (50 ov)

SUMMARY OF RESULTS

GROUP STAGE

Group A: England v India
at Birmingham – 29 May
India won by 63 runs.
India 232-8 (50 ov);
England 169 (45.2 ov)

Group A: Kenya v Sri Lanka
at Southampton – 30 May
Sri Lanka won by 45 runs.
Sri Lanka 275-8 (50 ov);
Kenya 230-6 (50 ov)

Group B: Bangladesh v Pakistan
at Northampton – 31 May
Bangladesh won by 62 runs.
Bangladesh 223-9 (50 ov);
Pakistan 161 (44.3 ov)

Group A: South Africa v Zimbabwe
at Chelmsford – 29 May
Zimbabwe won by 48 runs.
Zimbabwe 233-6 (50 ov);
South Africa 185 (47.2 ov)

Group B: Australia v West Indies
at Manchester – 30 May
Australia won by 6 wickets.
West Indies 110 (46.4 ov);
Australia 111-4 (40.4 ov)

Group B: Scotland v New Zealand
at Edinburgh – 31 May
New Zealand won by 6 wickets.
Scotland 121 (42.1 ov);
New Zealand 123-4 (17.5 ov)

SUPER SIX

Australia v India
at The Oval – 4 June
Australia won by 77 runs.
Australia 282-6 (50 ov);
India 205 (48.2 ov)

India v Pakistan
at Manchester – 8 June
India won by 47 runs.
India 227-6 (50 ov);
Pakistan 180 (45.3 ov)

Pakistan v Zimbabwe
at The Oval – 11 June
Pakistan won by 148 runs.
Pakistan 271-9 (50 ov);
Zimbabwe 123 (40.3 ov)

Pakistan v South Africa
at Nottingham – 5 June
South Africa won by 3 wickets.
Pakistan 220-7 (50 ov);
South Africa 221-7 (49 ov)

Australia v Zimbabwe
at Lord's – 9 June
Australia won by 44 runs.
Australia 303-4 (50 ov);
Zimbabwe 259-6 (50 ov)

India v New Zealand
at Nottingham – 12 June
New Zealand won by 5 wickets.
India 251-6 (50 ov);
New Zealand 253-5 (48.2 ov)

New Zealand v Zimbabwe
at Leeds – 6 June
No result.
Zimbabwe 175 (49.3 ov);
New Zealand 70-3 (15 ov)

New Zealand v South Africa
at Birmingham – 10 June
South Africa won by 74 runs.
South Africa 287-5 (50 ov);
New Zealand 213-8 (50 ov)

Australia v South Africa
at Leeds – 13 June
Australia won by 5 wickets.
South Africa 271-7 (50 ov);
Australia 272-5 (49.4 ov)

SUMMARY OF RESULTS

GROUP A

TEAM	POINTS	PLAYED	WON	LOSS	NO RESULT	RUN RATE	POINTS CARRIED FORWARD
South Africa	8	5	4	1	0	0.86	2
India	6	5	3	2	0	1.28	0
Zimbabwe	6	5	3	2	0	0.45	4
England	6	5	3	2	0	-0.33	NA
Sri Lanka	4	5	2	3	0	-0.81	NA
Kenya	0	5	0	5	0	-1.20	NA

GROUP B

TEAM	POINTS	PLAYED	WON	LOSS	NO RESULT	RUN RATE	POINTS CARRIED FORWARD
Pakistan	8	5	4	1	0	0.51	4
Australia	6	5	3	2	0	0.73	0
New Zealand	6	5	3	2	0	0.58	2
West Indies	6	5	3	2	0	0.50	NA
Bangladesh	4	5	2	3	0	-0.52	NA
Scotland	0	5	0	5	0	-1.93	NA

SUPER SIX TABLE

TEAM	POINTS	PLAYED	WON	LOSS	NO RE-SULT	RUN RATE	PCF
Pakistan	6	5	3	2	0	0.65	4
Australia	6	5	3	2	0	0.36	0
South Africa	6	5	3	2	0	0.17	2
New Zealand	5	5	2	2	1	-0.52	2
Zimbabwe	5	5	2	2	1	-0.79	4
India	2	5	1	4	0	-.015	–

Nick Dyer of Scotland celebrates with George Salmond after taking the wicket of Bangladesh's Khaled Mahmud at The Grange

1ST SEMI-FINAL

New Zealand v Pakistan
at Manchester – 16 June
Pakistan won by 9 wickets.
New Zealand 241-7 (50 ov);
Pakistan 242-1 (47.3 ov)

2ND SEMI-FINAL

Australia v South Africa
at Birmingham – 17 June
Match tied.
Australia 213 (49.2 ov);
South Africa 213 (49.4 ov)

FINAL

Australia v Pakistan
at Lord's – 20 June
Australia won by 8 wickets.
Pakistan 132 (39 ov);
Australia 133-2 (20.1 ov)

2003 South Africa, Zimbabwe & Kenya

Australian fans cheer as their team demolishes India in a one-sided final in Johannesburg

Aus-some

UNFORTUNATELY, the 2003 World Cup will be remembered for various controversies. England and New Zealand refused to play their respective matches in Zimbabwe and Kenya, citing security fears, and the matches were eventually awarded to host teams. The political situation in Zimbabwe and atrocities of the Robert Mugabe regime were brought to the fore, most emphatically by Andy Flower and Henry Olonga, who wore black arm bands during a match to protest the death of democracy under Mugabe's regime. Shane Warne tested positive in a drug test, a day before Australia's first match, and a few Indian players had to battle sponsorship issues back home before making it to the final World Cup squad.

ustralia were at the height of their power and the World Cup proved a cakewalk for a champion side. The reigns had been handed over from Steve Waugh to Ricky Ponting, and this unit won all of their 13 matches as they cruised to their third – and second successive – World Cup title and a $2 million kitty. India had played some exciting cricket to reach the summit, but they proved no match for Australia. Ponting simply demolished their attack, scoring 140 from 121 balls as Australia surged to a 125-run victory.

From an African perspective, it was disappointing that neither South Africa nor Zimbabwe qualified beyond the first round. South Africa, hosting their first international sports competition since the 1995 Rugby World Cup, were utterly disappointing. They lost their opening match – which included a splendid century from Brian Lara – by three runs, paying the price for a slow over rate, and remained dogged by inconsistency – the heavy defeat against New Zealand must still rankle – until Mark Boucher suffered a mind-block in a rain-affected match against Sri Lanka. The hosts, who had pumped so much into the organization of the event, were incapable of progressing to even the Super Six stage.

West Indies were unlucky not to progress, Pakistan never got going, Sri Lanka had an excellent start but then deteriorated, Bangladesh were very poor, and England paid the price for forfeiting their game against Zimbabwe. New Zealand rallied but folded, crucially against India, whose campaign, barring the final, was the stuff dreams are made of. Having lost to Australia, they strung together a memorable run of 10 wins from 12 matches until they ran into Ponting and Co. again. The fast bowling was overall very efficient and the batsmen lived up to expectations. Their win over Pakistan was one for ages and extended their dominance over their geographical neighbours to a fourth World Cup. In short, India were too good for everyone, bar Australia.

There were memorable moments: Sachin Tendulkar swept the Man-of-the-Series prize for his 673 runs in 11 matches, Chaminda Vaas netted 23 wickets from 10, Canada's John Davison slammed a record 67-ball century against West Indies, Kenya reached the semi-finals, and there were memorable centuries and bowling efforts along the way that enthralled fans. Overall, the tournament was deemed a success for its inventive style of coverage that led to increased viewer participation and a profit of $194 million was announced, a huge increase on the $51 million made in 1999, but the organization drew much criticism.

Overall, owing to Australia's bull run, there was a lingering feeling that this was a World Cup that should have delivered a lot more.

Chaminda Vaas appeals during the Super Six match between Sri Lanka and Zimbabwe

Opposite page: Brian Lara prepares to sweep the ball watched by Khaled Mashud of Bangladesh

John Davison's 67-ball century against West Indies was at the time the fastest World Cup ton.

GROUP A: SOUTH AFRICA, INDIA, ZIMBABWE, SRI LANKA, ENGLAND, KENYA

GROUP B: PAKISTAN, NEW ZEALAND, AUSTRALIA, WEST INDIES, BANGLADESH, SCOTLAND

2003 Wills World Cup statistics

Formats Round robin and Knockout
Host South Africa, Zimbabwe and Kenya
Champions Australia (third title)
Participants 12
Matches played 54
Attendance 626,845 (11,608 per match)
Most runs Sachin Tendulkar (673)
Most wickets Chaminda Vaas (23)

This was Canada's second World Cup appearance after 24 years. They had previously played in 1979.

Andrew Symonds in action during the match between Australia and Namibia

South Africa v West Indies

9 February

First match, Cape Town

BRIAN LARA walked out to the middle with West Indies in semi-crisis and was nearly walking back out a ball later. Makhaya Ntini drew an edge that Jacques Kallis, at second slip, floored. With a look to the skies and a deep breath, Lara summoned all his inner powers and put on a measured display. West Indies crawled to 30 after 15 overs before Lara hit the first six of the tournament, off Allan Donald no less, to cue a revival. Lara collected his fifty with consecutive fours in the 30th over and sailed into the nineties with a six and four in the 39th over. After a brief delay owing to cramps, Lara reached his 16th ODI century in the 42nd over. His second fifty needed just 43 balls and when he left, having scored his second World Cup century against South Africa, the Newlands crowd rose to applaud his achievement.

Australia v Pakistan

11 February

Fourth match, Johannesburg

THIS game saw an outstanding knock by a player once not scheduled to play this cracker of a contest between the 1999 World Cup finalists. Andrew Symonds was included in Australia's World Cup squad on a hunch by Ricky Ponting, and today the move paid off handsomely. Missing three key players, Australia were 86 for 4 when Symonds' hulking frame took guard against a revved-up Pakistan pace attack. Waqar Younis welcomed him with a bouncer and Symonds struggled to get going, very nearly chopping onto his stumps when 23. When Shoaib Akhtar sent back Ponting, Pakistan were threatening to turn this into a no-contest. A heated spat with Waqar, who sent down a beamer, brought out the beast in Symonds. Sixes began to flow from his broad bat; a robust cover drive off Waqar raised fifty, a cut off Shahid Afridi brought up a maiden ODI century. Symonds' last 36 deliveries yielded 49 runs and he finished on an Australian World Cup record of 143 off 125 balls. Later in the day he took a brilliant catch in the deep to cap Australia's 82-run win.

South Africa v New Zealand

16 February

Fifteenth match, Johannesburg

HAVING won just one of their previous 18 matches against South Africa, New Zealand looked like adding to that horrendous record when, chasing 306, they began their chase under lights. Stephen Fleming had been averaging 24 over his past 23 matches, but opening the innings, he chose the daunting cauldron that is The Wanderers to charge back into form. The overhead thunder and lightning were matched by some exhilarating stroke play from Fleming, who from the start launched into Makhaya Ntini and Shaun Pollock. Either side of a transitory power failure and two rain hold-ups, Fleming continued to bat with panache, peppering the midwicket and deep point boundaries with infallible regularity. Fleming's

The highest score after 15 overs in World Cup history is the 163 by Lara and Hinds against Canada.

dismissive handling of Donald, whose 5.5 overs went for 52, will live long in memory. South African shoulders drooped as Fleming clipped and cut his way to an unbeaten 134 from 132 balls, and a Duckworth-Lewis influenced victory was sealed by the Kiwi skipper when he cut Donald past backward point – where else? – and wrapped himself in a bear hug with his partner Nathan Astle.

Canada v West Indies

23 February

Twenty-fourth match, Centurion

JOHN DAVISON was unknown before this day, but after smashing a brilliant century off 67 balls – the then fastest in World Cup history – he forever etched his name in the record books. There were drops along the way, on 50 and 78, but never did Davison change his tempo: Mervyn Dillon was removed from the attack after just four overs, Vasbert Drakes lasted only two, Carl Hooper managed three, and the bowling was constantly shuffled in an attempt to curb Davison. Note Davison's role in the partnerships he forged: from 96 for the first wicket, Ishwar Maraj made 16; in 59 for the second, Desmond Chumney's contribution was 19. When Davison fell at a team score of 156, he had made 111.

Kenya v Sri Lanka

24 February

Twenty-sixth match, Nairobi

KENYA, one of four non-Test nations, pulled off the shock of the tournament with a remarkable 53-run victory against the Sri Lankans in Nairobi. After Kenya were thrashed by South Africa it seemed

John Davison of Canada hooks a six on his way to scoring the then fastest hundred in World Cup history

2003

Canada's 36 in 18.4 overs against SL is the lowest total and the shortest match in Cup history.

Ashish Nehra's effort against England in Durban was outstanding

they would fade into obscurity. But instead they rallied to defeat Sri Lanka, with Collins Obuya snaring 5 for 24, the best ever figures by a Kenyan. Sri Lanka were skittled 147 in 45 overs, chasing 211. Pool B was thrown alive by Kenya's highly unexpected victory over Sri Lanka and they kept their nerve against Canada and Bangladesh and, because of their four points over New Zealand, entered the Super Six stage with 10 out of a possible 12 points.

England v India

26 February

Thirtieth match, Durban

HAVING just managed to recover from a swollen ankle, the lanky left-arm pacer Ashish Nehra dismissed any doubts over his ability at this level with an awesome display under Kingsmead lights. India were defending 250, and England were 28 for 2 after 12 overs when Nehra was brought on. Running in like a man possessed, Nehra repeatedly landed the ball in the right spots and angled it across from across the wicket with unerring accuracy. In ten successive overs, Nehra ended with dream figures of 6 for 23, the best analysis by an Indian in World Cup history, and - until Glenn McGrath routed the Namibians a few days later – the best by anyone in a World Cup game outside of Headingley, the home of swing. 'He's had a swollen ankle for two days and it was sheer determination that made him play,' said his captain, Sourav Ganguly. 'He bowled a fantastic line. It's one of the

Tendulkar scored 52, 36, 81, 152, 50, 98, 5, 97, 15, 83 and 4 to bag a record 673 runs at 61.18.

best performances in a one-day international that I have seen since I started playing for India.'

Ashley Giles of England catches Matthew Hayden of Australia off the bowling of Andrew Caddick of England

India v Pakistan

1 March

Thirty-sixth match, Centurion

THE pinnacle of Sachin Tendulkar's amazing World Cup run was Centurion, in the cauldron of an India-Pakistan match. Tendulkar later recalled that he had not been able to sleep properly for 12 nights leading up to the match. India were chasing a stiff target, and Pakistan had a world-class pace attack. The tone was set in three deliveries of Shoaib Akhtar' opening over: a cut over third man for six, executed on tip-toes; a wristy clip past square leg for four; and a shuffled on-drive for four more. These three shots sent the crowd into a tizzy and paved the way for a famous victory, one that extended India's dominance over Pakistan in the World Cup. 'I got a couple of balls to hit, they went nicely off the bat, and things started happening,' was how Tendulkar recalled this innings two years later. 'Shoaib bowled short and wide. It was there to be hit, and I hit it well. It went for a six. I thought, this is working well so why not carry on?' There was no stopping Tendulkar thereafter, not until he cramped up and was dismissed for a splendid 98, fending off a short ball from Shoaib.

Australia v England

2 March

Thirty-seventh match, Port Elizabeth

AT Port Elizabeth on 2 March 2003, Andy Bichel dashed any hopes England might have had of sneaking into the Super Six. Having opted to bat, England raced away to 66 for 0 in ten overs, when Bichel, bowling first-change, started the rout. In eight deliveries, Bichel got Nick Knight to nick so slip, Michael Vaughan to edge behind, and bowled Nasser Hussain with a ripping outswinger. Four more wickets bundled out England and gave Bichel amazing figures of 10-0-20-7, but he wasn't done for the match. England rallied to reduce Australia to 135 for 8 when Bichel joined Michael Bevan, and what followed is the stuff of legend. The pair put on 73 runs – Bevan rotating the strike and Bichel thumping the ball everywhere – and England's World Cup dream was over. Bichel's unbeaten 34 to add to seven wickets was truly one of the great World Cup all-round efforts.

Australia's 256-run victory over Namibia is the biggest victory by runs.

THE SEMI-FINALS

Australia v Sri Lanka

18 March, First semi-final, Port Elizabeth

BY this time, there was little doubt that Australia were going to make it to the final, and another clinical performance made easy work of Sri Lanka by the time the Duckworth-Lewis method ruled in Australia's favour. Sri Lanka did well in bursts, especially against the vaunted top order, but Australia were indebted to an unbeaten 91 from Andrew Symonds, who got the score to 212 for 7. On a sluggish pitch, Brett Lee had the Sri Lankans in all sorts of trouble with his pace and bounce. What had looked an intriguing match at the halfway stage turned into complete demolition when Australia reduced Sri Lanka to 76 for 7; a 47-run alliance between Kumar Sangakkara and Chaminda Vaas was ended when the rain came, and with Sri Lanka well behind the asking rate at 123 for 7 in 38.1 overs, the D/L machinations had their say. This match will always be remembered for Adam Gilchrist's decision to walk, despite being reprieved by umpire Rudi Koertzen when he had edged an attempted sweep.

India v Kenya

20 March, Second semi-final, Durban

SOURAV GANGULY may not be one of the game's most liked characters, but few can question his batting ability. Having led his troops so commandingly since that first loss to Australia, Ganguly was also in form with the bat and scored his third century against Kenya, who had surprised many by reaching this far. In his 99th match as India captain, Ganguly began circumspectly but opened up finish on 111 from 114 balls; there was also a stroke-filled 83 from Sachin Tendulkar as India posted 270 for 4. In reply, Kenya didn't put up much of a fight – only Steve Tikolo, the captain, crossed 29 – and India brushed aside the minnows in a comprehensive 91-run win.

Opposite page: Sachin Tendulkar had a phenomenal run in 2003 but could not help India win the title

THE FINALS Australia v India 23 March, Johannesburg

FOR India, a much cherished dream came crashing down to earth at the Wanderers and, all the while, that mischievous smile rarely left Ricky Ponting's face as he led from the front, playing the innings of his life that powered Australia to 359 for 2 from 50 overs. After a sedate start, with Damien Martyn taking the initiative, Ponting burst open after reaching his fifty off 74 balls. First Harbhajan Singh was swung for two sixes, then an outrageous one-handed swipe off Ashish Nehra over square leg for six more. Ponting needed just 29 deliveries to get from 50 to 100, finishing with a stunning 140 from 121 balls. His eight sixes all flew over between long-on and square leg and that awesome display completely overshadowed Martyn's 84-ball 88 made with a broken finger.

Once Sachin Tendulkar was dismissed in the first over, bowled by Glenn McGrath, the match was over. Virender Sehwag hung around to score a brazen 82, with ten fours and three sixes, but a direct hit from Darren Lehmann cut him off. Two rain delays later, it was Lehmann would take the final catch of the match, ushering wild celebrations from the victorious Australians. It was their second successive World Cup victory, and seventeenth win in a row. There could not have been more deserving champions.

Kenya set the record for best performance by a non-Test playing nation after reaching the semis.

Ricky Ponting's unbeaten 140 from 121 balls is the highest individual score in a World Cup final.

FILA

‘Nothing was going to stop us’

Andy Bichel

World Cup winner and sixth-highest wicket-taker of the tournament

Australia's win in 2003 was a massive achievement for us, considering we had various distractions leading to the tournament. The loss of Shane Warne on the eve of the tournament was a big one, but everyone felt confident with his back-up, Brad Hogg, as he had played very well in the games leading to the World Cup. Brad actually added a lot more: in the field he was a star and when it came to his batting, Brad was always looking to improve his game every day. Andrew Symonds was another big player for us in 2003. His century against Pakistan was a real turning point for us.

The political turmoil in Zimbabwe probably pulled us even closer as a team. But once we arrived, it was fine. We even went to one of the farmer's houses for a barbeque, which relaxed the whole team. We played the game and won, which was most important. The crowd expressed their appreciation for us coming to Zimbabwe. We had done a lap of the field to thank them for their support that was really appreciated.

The game against England was a special one for me. I would always rank this one higher than the performance against New Zealand, because it was another opportunity that I had, since not too many opportunities came my way that often. I had been the 12th man so many times, and this time around I was bowling the best and was as fit as I could be. I really enjoyed the game against New Zealand as well, since it was a massive opportunity with the bat.

The Australian team had a never-say-die attitude, and this only came through winning games from tough positions. Invariably, someone would put their hands up when the chips were down and this trait became so powerful, that teams did not know what to do. Eventually, the belief in each other became so strong that every opposition was sought to be overcome through the collective effort of the team.

We were very confident going into the 2003 final. We wanted that World Cup so badly as a group that nothing was going to stop us. We had some golden years, but this team was very focused at the job ahead. The Indian team was playing reasonable cricket, but we had beaten it in the previous round and thus were not too anxious. There was only one man we were worried about, it also put immense pressure on him – Sachin Tendulkar. We had to get his wicket and as a bowling group we were all quite confident, so it did not really matter who would get his wicket. Then, from our side, Ricky Pointing played an amazing innings. I would be very surprised if it is ever matched in a World Cup final again. It was amazing.

Opposite page: Andy Bichel captures the wicket of Peter Ondongo during Australia's big win over Kenya

SUMMARY OF RESULTS

GROUP STAGE

Pool B: South Africa v West Indies
at Cape Town – 9 February
West Indies won by 3 runs.
West Indies 278-5 (50 ov);
South Africa 275-9 (49 ov)

Pool A: Zimbabwe v Namibia
at Harare – 10 February
Zimbabwe won by 86 runs.
Zimbabwe 340-2 (50 ov);
Namibia 104-5 (25.1 ov)

Pool B: New Zealand v Sri Lanka
at Bloemfontein – 10 February
Sri Lanka won by 47 runs.
Sri Lanka 272-7 (50 ov);
New Zealand 225 (45.3 ov)

Pool A: Australia v Pakistan
at Johannesburg – 11 February
Australia won by 82 runs.
Australia 310-8 (50 ov);
Pakistan 228 (44.3 ov)

Pool B: Bangladesh v Canada
at Durban – 11 February
Canada won by 60 runs.
Canada 180 (49.1 ov);
Bangladesh 120 (28 ov)

Pool A: India v Netherlands
at Paarl – 12 February
India won by 68 runs.
India 204 (48.5 ov);
Netherlands 136 (48.1 ov)

Pool B: South Africa v Kenya
at Potchefstroom – 12 February
South Africa won by 10 wickets.
Kenya 140 (38 ov);
South Africa 142-0 (21.2 ov)

Pool A: Zimbabwe v England
at Harare – 13 February
Zimbabwe won by a walkover.

Pool B: New Zealand v West Indies
at Port Elizabeth – 13 February
New Zealand won by 20 runs.
New Zealand 241-7 (50 ov);
West Indies 221 (49.4 ov)

Pool B: Bangladesh v Sri Lanka
at Pietermaritzburg – 14 February
Sri Lanka won by 10 wickets.
Bangladesh 124 (31.1 ov);
Sri Lanka 126-0 (21.1 ov)

Pool A: Australia v India
at Centurion – 15 February
Australia won by 9 wickets.
India 125 (41.4 ov);
Australia 128-1 (22.2 ov)

Pool B: Canada v Kenya
at Cape Town – 15 February
Kenya won by 4 wickets.
Canada 197 (49 ov);
Kenya 198-6 (48.3 ov)

Pool A: England v Netherlands
at East London – 16 February
England won by 6 wickets.
Netherlands 142-9 (50 ov);
England 144-4 (23.2 ov)

Pool A: Namibia v Pakistan
at Kimberley – 16 February
Pakistan won by 171 runs.
Pakistan 255-9 (50 ov);
Namibia 84 (17.4 ov)

Pool B: South Africa v New Zealand
at Johannesburg – 16 February
New Zealand won by 9 wickets.
South Africa 306-6 (50 ov);
New Zealand 229-1 (36.5 ov)

Pool B: Bangladesh v West Indies
at Benoni – 18 February
No result.
West Indies 244-9 (50 ov);
Bangladesh 32-2 (8.1 ov)

Pool A: England v Namibia
at Port Elizabeth – 19 February
England won by 55 runs.
England 272 (50 ov);
Namibia 217-9 (50 ov)

Pool A: Zimbabwe v India
at Harare – 19 February
India won by 83 runs.
India 255-7 (50 ov);
Zimbabwe 172 (44.4 ov)

Pool B: Canada v Sri Lanka
at Paarl – 19 February
Sri Lanka won by 9 wickets.
Canada 36 (18.4 ov);
Sri Lanka 37-1 (4.4 ov)

Pool A: Australia v Netherlands
at Potchefstroom – 20 February
Australia won by 75 runs.
Australia 170-2 (36 ov);
Netherlands 122 (30.2 ov)

Pool B: Kenya v New Zealand
at Nairobi – 21 February
Kenya won by a walkover.

Pool A: England v Pakistan
at Cape Town – 22 February
England won by 112 runs.
England 246-8 (50 ov);
Pakistan 134 (31 ov)

Pool B: South Africa v Bangladesh
at Bloemfontein – February 22,
South Africa won by 10 wickets.
Bangladesh 108 (35.1 ov);
South Africa 109-0 (12 ov)

Pool A: India v Namibia
at Pietermaritzburg – 23 February
India won by 181 runs.
India 311-2 (50 ov);
Namibia 130 (42.3 ov)

SUMMARY OF RESULTS

GROUP STAGE

Pool B: Canada v West Indies
at Centurion – 23 February
West Indies won by 7 wickets.
Canada 202 (42.5 ov);
West Indies 206-3 (20.3 ov)

Pool A: Zimbabwe v Australia
at Bulawayo – 24 February
Australia won by 7 wickets.
Zimbabwe 246-9 (50 ov);
Australia 248-3 (47.3 ov)

Pool B: Kenya v Sri Lanka
at Nairobi – 24 February
Kenya won by 53 runs.
Kenya 210-9 (50 ov);
Sri Lanka 157 (45 ov)

Pool A: Netherlands v Pakistan
at Paarl – 25 February
Pakistan won by 97 runs.
Pakistan 253-9 (50 ov);
Netherlands 156 (39.3 ov)

Pool A: England v India
at Durban – 26 February
India won by 82 runs.
India 250-9 (50 ov);
England 168 (45.3 ov)

Pool B: Bangladesh v New Zealand
at Kimberley – 26 February
New Zealand won by 7 wickets.
Bangladesh 198-7 (50 ov);
New Zealand 199-3 (33.3 ov)

Pool A: Australia v Namibia
at Potchefstroom – 27 February
Australia won by 256 runs.
Australia 301-6 (50 ov);
Namibia 45 (14 ov)

Pool B: South Africa v Canada
at East London – 27 February
South Africa won by 118 runs.
South Africa 254-8 (50 ov);
Canada 136-5 (50 ov)

Pool A: Zimbabwe v Netherlands
at Bulawayo – 28 February
Zimbabwe won by 99 runs.
Zimbabwe 301-8 (50 ov);
Netherlands 202-9 (50 ov)

Pool B: Sri Lanka v West Indies
at Cape Town – 28 February
Sri Lanka won by 6 runs.
Sri Lanka 228-6 (50 ov);
West Indies 222-9 (50 ov)

Pool A: India v Pakistan
at Centurion – 1 March
India won by 6 wickets.
Pakistan 273-7 (50 ov);
India 276-4 (45.4 ov)

Pool B: Bangladesh v Kenya
at Johannesburg – 1 March
Kenya won by 32 runs.
Kenya 217-7 (50 ov);
Bangladesh 185 (47.2 ov)

Pool A: Australia v England
at Port Elizabeth – 2 March
Australia won by 2 wickets.
England 204-8 (50 ov);
Australia 208-8 (49.4 ov)

Pool A: Namibia v Netherlands
at Bloemfontein – 3 March
Netherlands won by 64 runs.
Netherlands 314-4 (50 ov);
Namibia 250 (46.5 ov)

Pool B: Canada v New Zealand
at Benoni – 3 March
New Zealand won by 5 wickets.
Canada 196 (47 ov);
New Zealand 197-5 (23 ov)

Pool B: South Africa v Sri Lanka
at Durban – 3 March
Match tied.
Sri Lanka 268-9 (50 ov);
South Africa 229-6 (45 ov)

Pool A: Zimbabwe v Pakistan
at Bulawayo – 4 March
No result.
Pakistan 73-3 (14 ov)

Pool B: Kenya v West Indies
at Kimberley – 4 March
West Indies won by 142 runs.
West Indies 246-7 (50 ov);
Kenya 104 (35.5 ov)

SUMMARY OF RESULTS

SUPER SIX

Australia v Sri Lanka
at Centurion – 7 March
Australia won by 96 runs.
Australia 319-5 (50 ov);
Sri Lanka 223 (47.4 ov)

India v Kenya
at Cape Town – 7 March
India won by 6 wickets.
Kenya 225-6 (50 ov);
India 226-4 (47.5 ov)

New Zealand v Zimbabwe
at Bloemfontein – 8 March
New Zealand won by 6 wickets.
Zimbabwe 252-7 (50 ov);
New Zealand 253-4 (47.2 ov)

India v Sri Lanka
at Johannsburg – 10 March
India won by 183 runs.
India 292-6 (50 ov);
Sri Lanka 109 (23 ov)

Australia v New Zealand
at Port Elizabeth – 11 March
Australia won by 96 runs.
Australia 208-9 (50 ov);
New Zealand 112 (30.1 ov)

Kenya v Zimbabwe
at Bloemfontein – 12 March
Kenya won by 7 wickets.
Zimbabwe 133 (44.1 ov);
Kenya 135-3 (26 ov)

India v New Zealand
at Centurion – 14 March
India won by 7 wickets.
New Zealand 146 (45.1 ov);
India 150-3 (40.4 ov)

Australia v Kenya
at Durban – 15 March
Australia won by 5 wickets.
Kenya 174-8 (50 ov);
Australia 178-5 (31.2 ov)

Sri Lanka v Zimbabwe
at East London – 15 March
Sri Lanka won by 74 runs.
Sri Lanka 256-5 (50 ov);
Zimbabwe 182 (41.5 ov)

SUPER SIX TABLE

TEAM	POINTS	PLAYED	WON	LOSS	NO RESULT	RUN RATE	POINTS CARRIED FORWARD
Australia	24	3	3	0	0	1.85	12
India	20	3	3	0	0	0.89	8
Kenya	14	3	1	2	0	0.35	10
Sri Lanka	11.35	3	1	2	0	-0.84	7.5
New Zealand	8	3	1	2	0	-0.90	4
Zimbabwe	3.5	3	0	3	0	-1.25	3.5

INDIA

GROUP TABLE

GROUP A

TEAM	POINTS	PLAYED	WON	LOSS	NO RESULT	RUN RATE	POINTS CARRIED FORWARD
Australia	24	6	6	0	0	2.05	12
India	20	6	5	1	0	1.11	8
Zimbabwe	14	6	3	2	1	0.50	3.5
England	12	6	3	3	0	0.82	NA
Pakistan	10	6	2	3	1	0.23	NA
Netherlands	4	6	1	5	0	-1.45	NA
Namibia	0	6	0	6	0	-2.96	NA

GROUP TABLE

GROUP B

TEAM	POINTS	PLAYED	WON	LOSS	NO RESULT	TIE	RUN RATE	POINTS CARRIED FORWARD
Sri Lanka	18	6	4	1	0	1	1.20	7.5
Kenya	16	6	4	2	0	0	-0.69	10
New Zealand	16	6	4	2	0	0	0.99	4
South Africa	14	6	3	2	0	1	1.73	NA
West Indies	14	6	3	2	1	0	1.10	NA
Canada	4	6	1	5	0	0	-1.99	NA
Bangladesh	2	6	0	5	1	0	-2.05	NA

Andrew Symonds again came to the fore for Australia during the semi-final against Sri Lanka

1ST SEMI-FINAL
Australia v Sri Lanka at Port Elizabeth – 18 March
Australia won by 48 runs.
Australia 212-7 (50 ov);
Sri Lanka 123-7 (38.1 ov)

2ND SEMI-FINAL
India v Kenya at Durban – 20 March
India won by 91 runs.
India 270-4 (50 ov);
Kenya 179 (46.2 ov)

FINAL
Australia v India at Johannesburg – 23 March
Australia won by 125 runs.
Australia 359-2 (50 ov);
India 234 (39.2 ov)

2007 West Indies

Australia celebrate their third successive World Cup title

Blizzard of Oz

THE tournament organizers had hinted at changes to the format after South Africa misread the Duckworth-Lewis charts against Sri Lanka, but what transpired four years later in the Caribbean was an even more muddled and laborious World Cup. Spread across 47 days, the longest tournament ever, the cricket was often mediocre and the reaction from the locals muted. The 2007 World Cup lacked the distinctive Caribbean flavour that had been promised, was hit by controversy and the shock exit of India and Pakistan during the first round, and had to grapple with poor administration whose exorbitant pricing of tickets put many off.

As in 2003, Australia's domination meant this was another dour World Cup. India and Pakistan were ousted early, and the progress of Ireland and Bangladesh dashed the concept of the best eight teams of the world progressing to the Super Eight stage. The ICC's idea to schedule heavyweight clashes in the Super Eights on different days was proven horribly wrong, though, obviously, had India and Pakistan been there, it would have been a different story. And thus a seven-week long tournament was made to feel even longer with a series of mismatches.

Good moments were scarce. Herschelle Gibbs's six consecutive sixes, Lasith Malinga's four wickets in four deliveries, Tamim Iqbal's audacious innings against India, AB de Villiers' one-legged century, Mahela Jayawardene's silken innings against New Zealand and Adam Gilchrist's squash-ball-aided century in a farce of a final are moments that stand out.

Ultimately, the 2007 World Cup will be remembered for the horrible death of Bob Woolmer; and a string of resignations, retirements and sackings. It is a shame that the Caribbean carnival promised was never allowed to bloom.

Opposite page: Sri Lankan captain Mahela Jayawardene downed New Zealand with a masterful century in the semis

GROUP A: AUSTRALIA, SOUTH AFRICA, NETHERLANDS AND SCOTLAND

GROUP B: SRI LANKA, INDIA, BANGLADESH AND BERMUDA

GROUP A: NEW ZEALAND, ENGLAND, KENYA AND CANADA

GROUP B: WEST INDIES, IRELAND, ZIMBABWE AND PAKISTAN

2007 ICC World Cup statistics

Formats Round robin and Knockout
Host West Indies
Champions Australia (fourth title)
Participants 16
Matches played 51
Attendance 672,000 (13.176 per match)
Most runs Matthew Hayden (659)
Most wickets Glenn McGrath (26)

Matthew Hayden's 87 boundaries beat Sachin Tendulkar's record of 79.

The 172-run stand of Hayden and Gilchrist is the highest for the first wicket in a World Cup final.

Hershelle Gibbs became the first batsman in ODIs to hit six sixes in an over

Netherlands v South Africa

16 March

Seventh match, Basseterre

THE opposition bowling could hardly be described as challenging and the ground by no means the biggest, but six sixes in an over put Herschelle Gibbs into the record books. Gibbs' onslaught against Dan van Bunge was the first instance of such a feat in ODIs, and was just one passage of a severe drubbing the minnows were handed by South Africa. Wet weather delayed the start at Warner Park, but when play did get underway, it rained fours and sixes as South Africa amassed a monumental 353 in 40 overs. The first ball of the 30th over was swung over mid-on, the second driven over long-off, the third swung over midwicket, the fourth slogged to the same region, the fifth swatted over wide long-off and the sixth clubbed over deep midwicket.

Bangladesh v India

17 March

Eighth match, Trinidad

TAMIM IQBAL was catapulted into the limelight after he blitzed India during Bangladesh's upset win in the first week of the World Cup. India had arrived in the Caribbean with a much-vaunted squad and buoyed by coach Greg Chappell's promise of his 'Vision for 2007'. In 53 deliveries, Tamim sent those hopes crashing, with an assault for the ages. Bangladesh's bowlers, spearheaded by Mashrafe Mortaza, outdid themselves in restricting India to 191, and whatever confidence was left in India's reserves went out of the window with Tamim's stroke play. A blow to the neck when he missed a pull off Zaheer Khan left no imprint; Tamim's reply was to unleash an array of ravenous shots, the pick of which was a waltz down the track that resulted in Tamim slapping a pull over midwicket. That shot epitomized Bangladesh's spirit on the day. A government ban on public gatherings was forgotten in Bangladesh as thousands of jubilant fans partied into the night after this win.

Ireland v Pakistan

17 March

Ninth match, Jamaica

ON the same day as Bangladesh vanquished India, World Cup debutants Ireland gave their

There were seven instances of half-centuries in fewer than 30 deliveries.

countrymen a St Patrick's Day to remember. A sensational three-wicket win sent Pakistan crashing out of the World Cup and put Ireland in the lead of group D with three points – one more than West Indies and two ahead of Zimbabwe. Chasing a revised target of 128 from 47 overs in gloomy conditions, Ireland held their nerve to hit the jackpot with 32 balls to spare, when captain Trent Johnson smashed Azhar Mahmood over long-on for six. Ireland had bowled and fielded with purpose in helpful conditions to dismiss Pakistan for 132 in 45. four overs, with Boyd Rankin's three wickets cutting through a vaunted line-up, but they wobbled at the start of their innings. The innings was guided by Niall O'Brien, who hit an ODI-best 72 from 107 balls and shared valuable partnerships of 47 with William Porterfield for the third wicket, and 38 with his brother Kevin for the fifth wicket. It was a memorable day for cricket, no matter where one's allegiance lay.

The Ireland team made it a very special St. Patrick's Day by upsetting Pakistan

Bermuda v India

19 March
Twelfth match, Trinidad

AFTER the embarrassment against Bangladesh, India helped their cause of qualifying for Super Eights with a convincing all-round show against Bermuda. A sizzling eighth century from Virender Sehwag was the highlight of India's world-record 257-run win over the minnows in an important Group B encounter at Port of Spain. There were also sparkling half-centuries from Sourav Ganguly (89), Yuvraj Singh (83) and Sachin Tendulkar. India posted 413 for 5 in 50 overs – their all-time highest, top score of the World Cup history and fourth highest in all ODI cricket. The match began promisingly for Bermuda when Malachi Jones became the first bowler to take a wicket with his first delivery in a World Cup when he had Robin Uthappa spectacularly caught by Dwayne Leverock at slip, but India pillaged 203 runs in the last 20 overs and 136 in the last ten overs.

West Indies v Australia

27-28 March
Twenty-fifth match, Super Eights, Antigua

MATTHEW HAYDEN'S record-breaking display was the centrepiece of Australia's 322 for 6 after they'd lost the toss. Having needed 18 balls to open his account, Hayden provided a masterclass in how to pace a big score. It was a century of two distinct parts: he reached 58 off 80 balls and the next 100 he scored came from only 63. Hayden sparked into life during the eighth over, with consecutive boundaries off a luckless Jerome Taylor, was nearly run-out on 28, and efficiently batted on to three figures. Upon doing so, he promptly opened up: Taylor was smoked over long-on for six, driven over long-off for four and lofted for six more over long-on in consecutive deliveries. The caress was accompanied by a crash as Hayden steered and heaved Marlon Samuels for four and six, and the first ball after a brief rain delay was dumped

Australia set a new record of 300-plus scores in six straight ODI innings.

Lasith Malinga rocked South Africa with four wickets in four balls but was unable to secure victory
Opposite page: Mohammad Rafique was in the thick of action during Bangladesh's win over South Africa in the Super Eights

to long-off for four. Hayden's 158 from 143 balls, his second in as many matches, was the highest score by an Australian at the World Cup, surpassing the 143 not out made by Andrew Symonds in 2003, and the ninth best in the history of the tournament. It was fitting that the knock of this proportion came on a ground named after the legendary Sir Viv Richards.

South Africa v Sri Lanka

28 March
Twenty-sixth match, Super Eights, Guyana

SOUTH AFRICA somehow snuck home in a thriller that could have so easily been the biggest heist in ODI history. Set 210 to win, South Africa looked to be cruising as Jacques Kallis build on Graeme Smith's 59 to take the score along to 206 for 5, but Lasith Malinga's exceptional spell so nearly took Sri Lanka to the brink of victory. Firing in superb, full-length deliveries, Malinga ripped out South Africa's lower order. Shaun Pollock's leg stump was flattened by a full and straight slower ball; Andrew Hall spooned a yorker to cover; Kallis got back on strike for the hat-trick ball an over later only to edge a drive to Kumar Sangakkara; Makhaya Ntini was clueless to a vicious yorker. Malinga became the first bowler to take four wickets in four balls in international cricket, but it was all in vain as South African won, with Robin Peterson hitting the winning runs.

England v Sri Lanka

4 April
Thirty-third match, Super Eights, Antigua

IN this match, it all came down to the last ball. England needed three more runs against Sri Lanka, having pulled themselves back from a position of failure to the brink of an unlikely victory. Ravi Bopara was on 52 and faced Dilhara Fernando for the final ball of the match. Fernando pulled out of his run-up at the last minute and, at the second attempt, delivered and beat Bopara's bat to disturb the stumps. The thrilling win meant Sri Lanka had edged a thriller by two runs and moved closer to the semi-finals.

Bangladesh v South Africa

7 April
Thirty-fourth match, Super Eights, Guyana

BANGLADESH pulled off another shock victory, beating World No. 1 South Africa by 67 runs. Put in to bat, Bangladesh posted their best World Cup score to date of 251, with Mohammad Ashraful scoring 87. Apart from Andre Nel's 5 for 45 on return to the starting line-up, South Africa's bowling was patchy and Ashraful was able to repeatedly pull off the paddle shot, getting down on one knee and thrice connecting to send the ball over short fine leg. He took his time to start, but once he opened up, he was awesome to behold. In reply, South Africa had no answer to Bangladesh's medium-pace seam and spin attack, and were bowled out for 184 with eight balls left.

Herschelle Gibbs became the first man in ODIs to hit six sixes in an over, against Netherlands.

Matthew Hayden finished with 658 runs in 2007, 15 fewer than Sachin Tendulkar in 2003.

THE SEMI-FINALS

New Zealand v Sri Lanka

24 April, First semi-final, Jamaica

MAHELA JAYAWARDENE'S sublime hundred against New Zealand in the semi-final was an innings of pure genius: the Sri Lankan captain was unflappable and shed his inhibitions to expose a spectacular selection of strokes. It was in many ways the finest innings of the tournament, for it displayed aptly how to construct an ODI innings. That it came in the pressure situation of a semi-final commanded the respect of all. Jayawardene began cautiously, shoring up the attack and getting a feel for the surface. The first half of his innings was measured, with delicate dabs and nudges here and there, and once he had played himself in, Jayawardene made sure his was the centrepiece of an imposing total. Jayawardene went to his hundred, off 104 balls, with a superb late cut boundary against Oram before pulling Shane Bond for six as the bowler's last over went for 17. An unbeaten 115 showed the value of a well-paced innings after he'd taken 48 balls to score his first boundary. New Zealand were on course to challenge Sri Lanka's 289 for 5, but lost seven key wickets for 44 runs to slump from 105 for 2 to 149 for 9.

Australia v South Africa

25 April, Second semi-final, Gros Islet

IN the lead-up to this match, South Africa's coach Mickey Arthur had commented that the best way to stop an all-conquering Australia from clinching their third straight World Cup was to put the pressure on Ricky Ponting's team from the very first ball. That's easier said than done. On the day, South Africa's habit of choking when it mattered was once again to the fore; Australia's bowlers blew them away, reducing them to 27 for 5 before Justin Kemp's unbeaten 49 got them to 149. Australia's batsmen then needed just 18.3 overs to chase 150, Matthew Hayden (40) and Michael Clarke (60*) leading the way. Two-time defending champions had extended their 21-game winning streak and marched into yet another final.

Opposite page: Adam Gilchrist was simply outstanding as Australia trumped Sri Lanka in the controversial final in Barbados

THE FINALS Australia v Sri Lanka

28 April, Barbados

THIS was the day Sri Lanka were trumped by one man and his little squash ball. Australia had stormed into their fourth straight World Cup final and on the day Sri Lanka, deserved finalists, ran into Adam Gilchrist at his show-stopping best. With some help from a squash ball inserted into his left glove so that his bottom hand wouldn't be so dominant, Gilchrist scorched the highest score in a World Cup final, 149 from just 104 balls. It was an innings of pure control, beginning from the first ball facing which Gilchrist timed off the middle of his bat. For the next 129 minutes, the Sri Lankans were made to chase the ball as Gilchrist crisply struck the ball to all corners of the park in an assault reminiscent of Ponting's century against India in the previous final.. The tone was set in the second over, bowled by Chaminda Vaas, in which four and six were clubbed with ease. There was no looking back. Gilchrist might have had a quiet tournament until the final, but when it really mattered, he smoked 149 of the best runs ever.

However, the game ended in a farce, with Australia thinking the final was finished due to bad light after thirty-three overs of the Sri Lankan innings, in a match reduced by rain to 38 a side, only for play to resume in pitch darkness on a ground without floodlights.

Ponting (539) and Jayawardene (548) became the first captains to make more than 500 runs.

Dwayne Leverock's 1 for 96 against India were the most expensive figures in the World Cup.

'We had the perfect artillery'

Matthew Hayden

2007 World Cup winner and highest run-scorer of the tournament

THAT Australian team of 2007 was very focused on peaking towards the World Cup as any smart country, which meant that reaching milestones and targets, trialling combinations and permutations not reflected in the immediacy of the ICC's Future Tours Programme was our objective. Our strong belief as a one-day side was that the World Cup was still the pinnacle of the sporting calendar, a truly once in a life time opportunity to flex your country's collective muscle.

We had the perfect artillery. We had velocity with the ball, power with the bat, and we also had an incredible commitment – a collective commitment to our fielding efforts – which placed us as the best fielding side in the world. We were leaders in every sense which positioned us to be ahead of our time. In all three facets and disciplines of the game we were at our best.

Personally, I think that World Cup was a highlight in my one-day career. I had always felt like I had been a little disappointing in tournaments right from youth cricket and my last effort as a World Cup player, in 2003 in South Africa, wasn't up to the high standards I set myself. So I was very determined to have a good World Cup, and naturally extremely pleased that I was able to do so in such commanding fashion as the World Cup's highest run scorer.

That St Kitts innings, where I scored the fastest century in World Cup history, was very special. What was even more special was getting citizenship for Saint Kitts and Nevis, which of was a tremendous honour. And I think the final in Barbados, the way we started our innings, in particular the way that Adam Gilchrist completely took Sri Lanka out of play, was also amazing. And I think more than anything given the pending birth of Thomas, our last little boy, it was relief to get home in time to see him born.

Opposite page: Matthew Hayden was in outstanding form in 2007

As for Gilchrist's innings in the final, that was pretty much a duplicate of the previous World Cup final where he took India out of play in South Africa. He didn't make a century in that particular match but just the start was the key. To get Australia to a position of 0 for 100 off 10 overs in that particular final and then to start in a similar vein in 2007, it just completely demoralizes and crushes an opposition. So both of those were great innings.

As for the 2007 final itself, I guess a lot gets made of the way that it finished but the truth was that you can't beat the environment, and we tried to play it out as much as we possibly could. So just to finish from my point of view was a huge relief considering that Thomas, my son, was due on the day of the World Cup final.

Overall, I think the West Indies hosted a wonderful event. West Indians embrace cricket like no other in a very unique way – to them it is an enormous global event. However, I believe a 10-team format works far better than a 16-team format, a feature absent from the 2007 World Cup. A 10-team format makes for a shorter tournament and contributes to the quality of cricket. I think the one feature of the 2007 World Cup that was disappointing was the exorbitantly high ticket prices which proved exclusionary to the people of the Caribbean. The World Cup is an event which should benefit supporters of all nations, none more so than the host nation, and feasibility studies should be done ahead of such tournaments to facilitate such a recommendation. Moving forward, I believe - considering revenues generated from the gate are minuscule in comparison to sponsorship and media rights- that ticket prices should reflect the needs of our major stakeholders, the pundits.

SUMMARY OF RESULTS

GROUP STAGE

Pool D: West Indies v Pakistan
at Kingston – 13 March
West Indies won by 54 runs.
West Indies 241-9 (50 ov);
Pakistan 187 (47.2 ov)

Pool A: Australia v Scotland
at Basseterre – 14 March
Australia won by 203 runs.
Australia 334-6 (50 ov);
Scotland 131 (40.1 ov).

Pool C: Canada v Kenya
at Gros Islet – 14 March
Kenya won by 8 wickets.
Canada 199 (50 ov);
Kenya 203-3 (43.2 ov)

Pool B: Bermuda v Sri Lanka
at Port of Spain – 15 March
Sri Lanka won by 243 runs.
Sri Lanka 321-6 (50 ov);
Bermuda 78 (24.4 ov)

Pool D: Ireland v Zimbabwe
at Kingston – 15 March
Match tied.
Ireland 221-9 (50 ov);
Zimbabwe 221 (50 ov)

Pool C: England v New Zealand
at Gros Islet – 16 March
New Zealand won by 6 wickets.
England 209-7 (50 ov);
New Zealand 210/4 (41 ov)

Pool A: Netherlands v South Africa
at Basseterre – 16 March
South Africa won by 221 runs.
South Africa 353/3 (40/40 ov);
Netherlands 132/9 (40/40 ov)

Pool B: Bangladesh v India
at Port of Spain – 17 March
Bangladesh won by 5 wickets.
India 191 (49.3 ov);
Bangladesh 192/5 (48.3 ov)

Pool D: Ireland v Pakistan
at Kingston – 17 March
Ireland won by 3 wickets.
Pakistan 132 (45.4 ov);
Ireland 133/7 (41.4/47 ov)

Pool A: Australia v Netherlands
at Basseterre – 18 March
Australia won by 229 runs.
Australia 358/5 (50 ov);
Netherlands 129 (26.5 ov)

Pool C: Canada v England
at Gros Islet – 18 March
England won by 51 runs.
England 279/6 (50 ov);
Canada 228/7 (50 ov)

Pool B: Bermuda v India
at Port of Spain – 19 March
India won by 257 runs.
India 413/5 (50 ov);
Bermuda 156 (43.1 ov)

Pool D: West Indies v Zimbabwe
at Kingston – 19 March
West Indies won by 6 wickets.
Zimbabwe 202/5 (50 ov);
West Indies 204/4 (47.5 ov)

Pool C: Kenya v New Zealand
at Gros Islet – 20 March
New Zealand won by 148 runs.
New Zealand 331/7 (50 ov);
Kenya 183 (49.2 ov)

Pool A: Scotland v South Africa
at Basseterre – 20 March
South Africa won by 7 wickets.
Scotland 186/8 (50 ov);
South Africa 188/3 (23.2 ov)

Pool B: Bangladesh v Sri Lanka
at Port of Spain – 21 March
Sri Lanka won by 198 runs.
Sri Lanka 318/4 (50 ov);
Bangladesh 112 (37/46 ov)

Pool D: Pakistan v Zimbabwe
at Kingston – 21 March
Pakistan won by 93 runs.
Pakistan 349 (49.5 ov);
Zimbabwe 99 (19.1/20 ov)

Pool C: Canada v New Zealand
at Gros Islet – 22 March
New Zealand won by 114 runs.
New Zealand 363/5 (50 ov);
Canada 249 (49.2 ov)

Pool A: Netherlands v Scotland
at Basseterre – 22 March
Netherlands won by 8 wickets.
Scotland 136 (34.1 ov);
Netherlands 140/2 (23.5 ov)

Pool B: India v Sri Lanka
at Port of Spain – 23 March
Sri Lanka won by 69 runs.
Sri Lanka 254/6 (50 ov);
India 185 (43.3 ov)

Pool D: West Indies v Ireland
at Kingston – 23 March
West Indies won by 8 runs.
Ireland 183/8 (48/48 ov);
West Indies 190/2 (38.1/48 ov)

Pool A: Australia v South Africa
at Basseterre – 24 March
Australia won by 83 runs.
Australia 377/6 (50 ov);
South Africa 294 (48 ov)

Pool C: England v Kenya
at Gros Islet – 24 March
England won by 7 wickets.
Kenya 177 (43/43 ov);
England 178/3 (33/43 ov)

Pool B: Bangladesh v Bermuda
at Port of Spain – 25 March
Bangladesh won by 7 wickets.
Bermuda 94/9 (21/21 ov);
Bangladesh 96/3 (17.3/21 ov)

SUMMARY OF RESULTS

SUPER EIGHTS

West Indies v Australia
at North Sound – 27-28 March
Australia won by 103 runs.
Australia 322/6 (50 ov);
West Indies 219 (45.3 ov)

South Africa v Sri Lanka
at Providence – 28 March
South Africa won by 1 wicket.
Sri Lanka 209 (49.3 ov);
South Africa 212/9 (48.2 ov)

West Indies v New Zealand
at North Sound – 29 March
New Zealand won by 7 wickets.
West Indies 177 (44.4 ov);
New Zealand 179/3 (39.2 ov)

England v Ireland
at Providence – 30 March
England won by 48 runs.
England 266/7 (50 ov);
Ireland 218 (48.1 ov)

Australia v Bangladesh
at North Sound – 31 March
Australia won by 10 wickets.
Bangladesh 104/6 (22/22 ov);
Australia 106/0 (13.5/22 ov)

West Indies v Sri Lanka
at Providence – 1 April
Sri Lanka won by 113 runs.
Sri Lanka 303/5 (50 ov);
West Indies 190 (44.3 ov)

Bangladesh v New Zealand
at North Sound – 2 April
New Zealand won by 9 wickets.
Bangladesh 174 (48.3 ov);
New Zealand 178/1 (29.2 ov)

Ireland v South Africa
at Providence – 3 April
South Africa won by 7 wickets.
Ireland 152/8 (35/35 ov);
South Africa 165/3 (31.3/35 ov)

England v Sri Lanka
at North Sound – 4 April 2007
Sri Lanka won by 2 runs.
Sri Lanka 235 (50 ov);
England 233/8 (50 ov)

Bangladesh v South Africa
at Providence – 7 April 2007
Bangladesh won by 67 runs.
Bangladesh 251/8 (50 ov);
South Africa 184 (48.4 ov)

Australia v England
at North Sound – 8 April 2007
Australia won by 7 wickets.
England 247 (49.5 ov);
Australia 248/3 (47.2 ov)

Ireland v New Zealand
at Providence – 9 April 2007
New Zealand won by 129 runs.
New Zealand 263/8 (50 ov);
Ireland 134 (37.4 ov)

West Indies v South Africa
at St George's – 10 April
South Africa won by 67 runs.
South Africa 356/4 (50 ov);
West Indies 289/9 (50 ov)

Bangladesh v England
at Bridgetown – 11 April
England won by 4 wickets.
Bangladesh 143 (37.2 ov);
England 147/6 (44.5 ov)

New Zealand v Sri Lanka
at St George's – 12 April
Sri Lanka won by 6 wickets.
New Zealand 219/7 (50 ov);
Sri Lanka 222/4 (45.1 ov)

Australia v Ireland
at Bridgetown – 13 April
Australia won by 9 wickets.
Ireland 91 (30 ov);
Australia 92/1 (12.2 ov)

New Zealand v South Africa
at St George's – 14 April 2007
New Zealand won by 5 wickets.
South Africa 193/7 (50 ov);
New Zealand 196/5 (48.2 ov)

Bangladesh v Ireland
at Bridgetown – 15 April 2007
Ireland won by 74 runs.
Ireland 243/7 (50 ov);
Bangladesh 169 (41.2 ov)

Australia v Sri Lanka
at St George's – 16 April 2007
Australia won by 7 wickets.
Sri Lanka 226 (49.4 ov);
Australia 232/3 (42.4 ov)

England v South Africa
at Bridgetown – 17 April 2007
South Africa won by 9 wickets.
England 154 (48 ov);
South Africa 157/1 (19.2 ov)

Ireland v Sri Lanka
at St George's – 18 April
Sri Lanka won by 8 wickets.
Ireland 77 (27.4 ov);
Sri Lanka 81/2 (10 ov)

West Indies v Bangladesh
at Bridgetown – 19 April
West Indies won by 99 runs.
West Indies 230/5 (50 ov);
Bangladesh 131 (43.5 ov)

Australia v New Zealand
at St George's – 20 April
Australia won by 215 runs.
Australia 348/6 (50 ov);
New Zealand 133 (25.5 ov)

West Indies v England
at Bridgetown – 21 April
England won by 1 wicket.
West Indies 300 (49.5 ov);
England 301/9 (49.5 ov)

SUMMARY OF RESULTS

GROUP A

TEAM	POINTS	PLAYED	WON	LOSS	NO RESULT	NET RUN RATE
Australia	6	3	3	0	0	+3.33
South Africa	4	3	2	1	0	+2.403
Netherlands	2	3	1	2	0	-2.527
Scotland	0	3	0	3	0	-3.793

GROUP B

TEAM	POINTS	PLAYED	WON	LOSS	NO RESULT	TIE	RUN RATE
Sri Lanka	6	3	3	0	0	0	+3.493
Bangladesh	4	3	2	1	0	0	-1.523
India	2	3	1	2	0	0	+1.206
Bermuda	0	3	0	3	0	0	-4.345

GROUP C

TEAM	POINTS	PLAYED	WON	LOSS	NO RESULT	NET RUN RATE
New Zealand	6	3	3	0	0	+2.138
England	4	3	2	1	0	+0.418
Kenya	2	3	1	2	0	-1.194
Canada	0	3	0	3	0	-1.389

GROUP D

TEAM	POINTS	PLAYED	WON	LOSS	NO RESULT	TIE	NET RUN RATE
West Indies	6	3	3	0	0	0	+0.764
Ireland	3	3	1	1	0	1	-0.092
Pakistan	2	3	1	2	0	0	+0.089
Zimbabwe	1	3	0	2	0	1	-0.886

SUMMARY OF RESULTS

SUPER EIGHTS TABLE						
TEAM	POINTS	PLAYED	WON	LOSS	NO RESULT	NET RUN RATE
Australia	14	7	7	0	0	+2.4
Sri Lanka	10	7	5	2	0	+1.483
New Zealand	10	7	5	2	0	+0.253
South Africa	8	7	4	3	0	+0.313
England	6	7	3	4	0	-0.394
West Indies	4	7	2	5	0	-0.566
Bangladesh	2	7	1	6	0	-1.514
Ireland	2	7	1	6	0	-1.73

AB de Villiers dives back into his crease during South Africa's exit in the semis

1ST SEMI-FINAL

New Zealand v Sri Lanka at Kingston – 24 April
Sri Lanka won by 81 runs.
Sri Lanka 289/5 (50 ov);
New Zealand 208 (41.4 ov)

2ND SEMI-FINAL

Australia v South Africa at Gros Islet – 25 April
Australia won by 7 wickets.
South Africa 149 (43.5 ov);
Australia 153/3 (31.3 ov)

FINAL

Australia v Sri Lanka at Bridgetown – 28 April
Australia won by 53 runs.
Australia 281/4 (38/38 ov);
Sri Lanka 215/8 (36/36 ov)

WORLD CUP RECORDS

WORLD CUP FINALISTS

SEASON	VENUES	TROPHY	WINNERS	RUNNERS-UP
1975	England	Prudential Cup	West Indies	Australia
1979	England	Prudential Cup	West Indies	England
1983	England	Prudential Cup	India	West Indies
1987	India/Pakistan	Reliance Cup	Australia	England
1992	Australia/New Zealand	B&H World Cup	Pakistan	England
1996	India/Pakistan/Sri Lanka	Wills World Cup	Sri Lanka	Australia
1999	England/Scotland/Ireland/Holland	ICC World Cup	Australia	Pakistan
2003	South Africa/Zimbabwe/Kenya	ICC World Cup	Australia	India
2007	West Indies	ICC World Cup	Australia	Sri Lanka

TEAM RECORDS

SUMMARY OF RESULTS

TEAM	MATCHES	WON	LOST	NR	TIED	SUCCESS
Australia	69	51	17	0	1	74.63%
Bangladesh	20	5	14	1	0	26.31%
Bermuda	3	0	3	0	0	0.00
Canada	12	1	11	0	0	8.33%
East Africa	3	0	3	0	0	0.00
England	59	36	22	1	0	62.06%
India	58	32	25	1	0	56.14%
Ireland	9	2	6	0	1	27.77%
Kenya	23	6	16	1	0	27.77%
Namibia	6	0	6	0	0	0.00
Netherlands	14	2	12	0	0	14.28%
New Zealand	62	35	26	1	0	57.37%
Pakistan	56	30	24	2	0	55.55%

SUMMARY OF RESULTS

TEAM	MATCHES	WON	LOST	NR	TIED	SUCCESS
Scotland	8	0	8	0	0	0.00
South Africa	40	25	13	2	0	65.00%
Sri Lanka	57	25	30	1	1	45.53%
UAE	5	1	4	0	0	20.00%
West Indies	57	35	21	1	0	62.50%
Zimbabwe	45	8	33	3	1	20.23%

PLAYING RECORD OF EACH TEAM

TEAM	RUNS	AVG	RPO	WICKETS	AVG	RPO	HS	LS
Australia	15938	37.50	5.05	569	24.16	4.38	377	129
New Zealand	13245	32.07	4.65	445	29.94	4.39	363	112
India	12870	32.91	4.77	433	27.66	4.37	413	125
England	12520	32.26	4.53	463	25.40	4.08	334	93
Pakistan	12421	31.28	4.56	424	27.05	4.36	349	74
West Indies	12222	31.66	4.52	441	26.19	4.15	360	93
Sri Lanka	12018	29.74	4.61	376	33.34	4.84	398	86
South Africa	8899	37.39	5.05	302	26.06	4.37	356	149
Zimbabwe	8436	24.52	4.12	248	37.33	4.81	340	99
Kenya	4154	24.15	4.05	132	36.46	4.93	254	104
Bangladesh	3023	18.21	3.86	111	32.17	4.67	251	108
Netherlands	2420	22.00	3.97	81	42.64	5.71	314	122
Canada	1912	17.38	3.54	54	39.79	5.39	249	36
Ireland	1452	18.37	3.94	53	29.79	4.79	243	77
Scotland	1153	15.58	3.46	36	41.19	5.49	186	68
Namibia	830	15.37	4.23	33	54.33	5.97	250	45
UAE	784	20.10	3.41	22	48.40	5.32	220	136
East Africa	342	12.21	2.03	10	72.20	4.81	128	94
Bermuda	328	11.31	3.69	14	59.28	7.06	156	78

MOST WICKETS IN A WORLD CUP

PLAYER	SEASON	M	O	R	W	BBI	AVG	ECONOMY	S/R-
G. McGrath	2007	11	80.5	357	26	3/14	13.73	4.41	18.6
C. Vaas	2003	10	88	331	23	6/25	14.39	3.76	22.9
M. Muralitharan	2003	10	84.4	351	23	4/19	15.26	4.14	22.0
S. Tait	2007	11	84.3	467	23	4/39	20.30	5.52	22.0
B. Lee	2003	10	83.1	394	22	5/42	17.90	4.73	22.6
G. McGrath	2003	11	87	310	21	7/15	14.76	3.56	24.8
B. Hogg	2007	11	82.5	332	21	4/27	15.80	4.00	23.6
G. Allott	1999	9	87.4	325	20	4/37	16.25	3.70	26.3
S. Warne	1999	10	94.2	361	20	4/29	18.66	3.81	29.3
S. Malinga	2007	8	58.2	284	18	4/54	15.77	4.86	19.4
R. Binny	1983	8	88	336	18	4/29	18.66	3.81	29.3
W. Akram	1992	10	89.4	338	18	4/32	18.77	3.76	29.8
C. McDermott	1987	8	73	341	18	5/44	18.94	4.67	24.3
G. McGrath	1999	10	95.4	367	18	5/14	20.38	3.83	31.8
Z. Khan	2003	11	88.2	374	18	4/42	20.77	4.23	29.4

MOST RUNS IN A WORLD CUP

PLAYER	SEASON	M	I	NO	R	HS	AVG	BF	SR	100	50
S. Tendulkar	2003	11	11	0	673	152	61.18	754	89.25	1	6
M. Hayden	2007	11	10	1	659	158	73.22	652	101.07	3	1
M. Jayawardene	2007	11	11	2	548	115*	60.88	644	85.09	1	4
R. Ponting	2007	11	9	1	539	113	67.37	565	95.39	1	4
S. Tendulkar	1996	7	7	1	523	137	87.16	609	85.87	2	3
S. Styris	2007	10	9	3	499	111*	83.16	598	83.44	1	4
J. Kallis	2007	10	9	3	485	128*	80.83	578	83.91	1	3
M. Waugh	1996	7	7	1	484	130	80.66	563	85.96	3	1
G. Gooch	1987	8	8	0	471	115	58.87	670	70.29	1	3
S. Jayasuriya	1996	11	11	1	467	115	46.70	475	98.31	2	2

Neil Johnson of Zimbabwe celebrates a wicket during the 1999 World Cup match against South Africa at Chelmsford

HIGHEST INNINGS TOTAL FOR EACH TEAM

413-5 in 50 overs	India v Bermuda at Port of Spain	2007
398-5 in 50 overs	Sri Lanka v Kenya at Kandy	1996
377-6 in 50 overs	Australia v South Africa at Basseterre	2007
363-5 in 50 overs	New Zealand v Canada at Gros Islet	2007
360-4 in 50 overs	West Indies v Pakistan at Karachi	1987
356-4 in 50 overs	South Africa v West Indies at St George's	2007
340-2 in 50 overs	Zimbabwe v Namibia at Harare	2003
334-4 in 60 overs	England v India at Lord's	1975
314-4 in 50 overs	Netherlands v Namibia at Bloemfontein	2003
254-7 in 50 overs	Kenya v Sri Lanka at Kandy	1996
251-8 in 50 overs	Bangladesh v South Africa at Guyana	2007
250-4 in 50 overs	Namibia v Netherlands at Bloemfontein	2003
220-3 in 49.5 overs	UAE v Netherlands at Lahore	1996
202 in 42.5 overs	Canada v West Indies at Centurion	2003
181-7 in 50 overs	Scotland v Australia at Worcester	1999
128-8 in 60 overs	East Africa v New Zealand at Birmingham	1975

LOWEST INNINGS TOTAL FOR EACH TEAM

36 in 18.4 overs	Canada v Sri Lanka at Paarl	2003
45 in 14 overs	Namibia v Australia at Potchef-stroom	2003
68 in 31.3 overs	Scotland v West Indies at Leicester	1999
74 in 40.2 overs	Pakistan v England at Adelaide	1992
86 in 37.2 overs	Sri Lanka v West Indies at Manchester	1975
93 in 36.2 overs	England v Australia at Leeds	1975
93 in 35.2 overs	West Indies v Kenya at Pune	1996
94 in 52.3 overs	East Africa v England at Birmingham	1975
104 in 35.5 overs	Kenya v West Indies at Kimberley	2003
108 in 35.1 overs	Bangladesh v South Africa at Bloemfontein	2003
109-9 in 33 overs	UAE v Pakistan at Peshawar	1996
112 in 30.1 overs	New Zealand v Austra-lia at Port Elizabeth	2003
120-8 in 34.1 overs	India v Sri Lanka at Calcutta	1996
122 in 30.2 overs	Netherlands v Austra-lia at Potchefstroom	2003

LARGEST MARGINS OF VICTORY

BY RUNS

257 runs	India beat Bermuda at Port of Spain	2007
256 runs	Australia beat India at Lord's	1975
243 runs	SL beat Bermuda at Port of Spain	2007
229 runs	Aus beat Netherlands at Basseterre	2007
221 runs	SA beat Netherlands at Basseterre	2007
215 runs	Australia beat NZ at St George's	2007
203 runs	Australia beat Scotland at Basseterre	2007
202 runs	England beat India at Lord's	1975
198 runs	SL beat Bangladesh at Port of Spain	2007
196 runs	England beat East Africa at Birmingham	1975
192 runs	Pakistan v Sri Lanka at Nottingham	1975
191 runs	West Indies v Sri Lanka at Karachi	1987
183 runs	India v Sri Lanka at Johannesbury	2003
181 runs	NZ v Namibia at Pietermaritzburg	2003
171 runs	Pakistan v Namibia at Kimberley	2003
169 runs	South Africa v UAE at Rawalpindi	1996
162 runs	Australia v India at Nottingham	1983
160 runs	SA v Netherlands at Rawalpindi	1996
157 runs	India v Sri Lanka at Taunton	1999
148 runs	Pakistan v Zimbabwe at The Oval	1999
148 runs	New Zealand v Kenya at Gros Islet	2007
144 runs	Sri Lanka v Kenya at Kandy	1996
142 runs	West Indies v Kenya at Kimberley	2003
129 runs	New Zealand v Ireland at Providence	2007
128 runs	Australia v Zimbabwe at Hobart	1992
125 runs	Australia v India at Johannesburg	2003
122 runs	South Africa v England at The Oval	1999
119 runs	NZ v Netherlands at Vadodara	1996

BY WICKETS

10 wickets	India beat East Africa at Leeds	1975
	WI beat Zimbabwe at Birmingham	1983
	WI beat Pakistan at Melbourne	1992
	SA beat Kenya at Potchefstroom	2003
	SL beat Bangladesh at Pietermaritzburg	2003
	SA beat Bangladesh at Bloemfontein	2003
	Australia beat Bangladesh at North Sound	2007
9 wickets	West Indies beat SL at Manchester	1975
	WI beat India at Birmingham	1975
	NZ beat Sri Lanka at Nottingham	1979
	England beat Sri Lanka at Leeds	1983
	India beat NZ at Nagpur	1987
	SA beat Australia at Sydney	1992
	Pakistan beat UAE at Rawalpindi	1996
	England beat Kenya at Canterbury	1999
	Pakistan beat NZ at Manchester	1999
	Aus beat India at Pietermaritzburg	2003
	NZ beat SA at Johannesburg	2003
	Sri Lanka beat Canada at Paarl	2003
	NZ beat Bangladesh at North Sound	2007
	Australia beat Ireland at Bridgetown	2007
	SA beat England at Bridgetown	2007

BY RUNS		
1 run	Australia beat India at Madras	1987
1 run	Australia beat India at Brisbane	1992
2 runs	Sri Lanka beat England at North Sound	2007
3 runs	New Zealand beat India at Hyderabad	1987
3 runs	Australia beat New Zealand at Indore	1987
3 runs	Australia beat India at Leicester	1999
3 runs	West Indies beat South Africa at Cape Town	2003
5 runs	Australia beat West Indies at Mohali	1996
6 runs	Sri Lanka beat West Indies at Cape Town	2003
7 runs	Australia beat India at Calcutta	1987
9 runs	England beat New Zealand at Manchester	1979
9 runs	Zimbabwe beat England at Albury	1992
9 runs	England beat India at Perth	1992
10 runs	Pakistan beat Australia at Leeds	1999

BY WICKETS		
1 wicket	WI beat Pakistan at Birmingham	1975
1 wicket	Pakistan beat West Indies at Lahore	1987
1 wicket	South Africa beat Sri Lanka at Providence	2007
1 wicket	England beat West Indies at Bridgetown	2007
2 wickets	NZ beat England at Birmingham	1983
2 wickets	Eng beat Australia at Gujranwala	1987
2 wickets	Pakistan beat Australia at Leeds	2003
2 wickets	Australia beat England at Port Elizabeth	2003

FASTEST HUNDREDS

66 balls	Matthew Hayden (Australia) v South Africa at St Kitts	2007
67 balls	John Davison (Canada) v West Indies at Centurion	1975
72 balls	Kapil Dev (India) v Zimbabwe at Tunbridge Wells	1983
72 balls	Adam Gilchrist (Australia) v Sri Lanka at Barbados	2007
81 balls	Virender Sehwag (India) v Bermuda at Port of Spain	2007
82 balls	Clive Lloyd (West Indies) v Australia at Lord's	1975
82 balls	Brad Hodge (Australia) v Netherlands at St Kitts	2007
83 balls	Brian Lara (West Indies) v South Africa at Karachi	1996
84 balls	Sachin Tendulkar (India) v Kenya at Bristol	1999
85 balls	Sunil Gavaskar (India) v New Zealand at Nagpur	1987
85 balls	Ricky Ponting (Australia) v Scotland at St Kitts	2007
85 balls	Sanath Jayasuriya (Sri Lanka) v Bangladesh at Trinidad	2007

FASTEST FIFTIES

20 balls	Brendon McCullum (New Zealand) v Canada at St Lucia	2007
21 balls	Mark Boucher (South Africa) v Netherlands at St Kitts	2007
22 balls	Mark Boucher (South Africa) v West Indies at St George's	2007
23 balls	Brian Lara (West Indies) v Canada at Centurion	2003
24 balls	Wavell Hinds (West Indies) v Canada at Centurion	2003
25 balls	John Davison (Canada) v West Indies at Centurion	1975
25 balls	Andy Blignaut (Zimbabwe) v Australia at Bulawayo	2003

MOST EXTRAS IN AN INNINGS (40 OVERS OR MORE)

59 Extras	by Scotland v Pakistan at Chester-Le-Street	1999
51 Extras	by India v Zimbabwe at Leicester	1999
47 Extras	by Pakistan v New Zealand at Manchester	1999
44 Extras	by India v Kenya at Bristol	1999
44 Extras	by Scotland v Bangladesh at Edinburgh	1999
42 Extras	by Pakistan v New Zealand at Christchurch	1999
40 Extras	by Pakistan v England at Rawalpindi	1987
40 Extras	by Pakistan v New Zealand at Northampton	1999
40 Extras	by Pakistan v Netherlands at Paarl	2003

PHOTO CREDITS

CORBIS: 76, 79, 83, 85, 86-87, 126, 130

GETTY IMAGES: 18, 50, 51, 54, 58-59, 61, 62, 63, 65, 70-71, 72, 73, 74, 75, 77, 80, 88, 89, 90, 91, 92, 93, 95, 96, 101, 102-103, 104, 105, 106, 107, 108, 109, 111, 112, 117, 119, 120-121, 123, 124, 125, 127, 129, 135, 142

PATRICK EAGAR: 2, 6, 10-11, 12-13, 15, 16, 20, 21, 22-23, 25, 26, 27, 29, 30, 32, 33, 34-35, 37, 38, 39 (all), 41, 42, 45, 46-47, 49, 53, 57, 66